How We Impact the Environment

Grades 5-8

Written by Krystal Lapierre
Illustrated by Dan Day and S&S Learning Materials

About the author:
Krystal Lapierre has been involved in teaching science to children in a variety of settings for almost three years. Krystal's academic qualifications include a Master's degree in biology and a Bachelor of Science. She is presently teaching in Korea.

ISBN 978-1-55035-926-8
Copyright 2008

Published in the U.S.A by:
On The Mark Press
3909 Witmer Road PMB 175
Niagara Falls, New York
14305
www.onthemarkpress.com

Published in Canada by:
S&S Learning Materials
15 Dairy Avenue
Napanee, Ontario
K7R 1M4
www.sslearning.com

At A Glance

Learning Expectations	Student Booklet	Reading Information Activities	Investigation Activities	Language Activities	Thinking Activities	Research Activities	Review
Understanding concepts							
Recognize environmental issues	•	•	•	•	•	•	
Understand the impacts people have on the environment	•	•	•		•	•	•
Be aware of energy usage and waste	•				•	•	•
Help spread public awareness about environmental issues	•		•		•		
Research important environmental information	•			•	•	•	•
Understand the importance of caring for and protecting our environment	•				•		•
Skills of inquiry, design, and communication							
Demonstrate an understanding of the scientific method by following the steps for experimentation, and recording the procedures and observations			•		•	•	
Use appropriate vocabulary to describe environmental issues			•	•		•	
Formulate questions and seek answers	•		•		•	•	•
Record observations, findings, and measurements using drawings, charts, and written descriptions	•		•		•	•	
Demonstrate problem-solving skills and creativity		•	•		•	•	
Relating science and technology to the outside world							
Synthesize information	•	•	•		•	•	
Recognize the main idea	•	•	•		•		
Research facts/definitions				•	•	•	•
Distinguish between opinion and fact		•		•	•		
Debate controversial topics					•		•
Illustrate creatively	•				•	•	•
Innovate designs and creative solutions to problems	•	•			•	•	•
Help spread public awareness about environmental issues	•		•		•		
Make inferences	•	•	•		•	•	•

Table of Contents

At A Glance™ 2

Teacher Rubric 5

Student Rubric 6

Introduction 7

Materials List 8

INTRODUCTION TO HUMAN IMPACTS ON THE ENVIRONMENT

What Impact Are We Having? (Grades 5-8) 10

Environmental Dictionary (Grades 5-8) 14

Ecological Footprint (Grades 5-8) 15

Positive, Negative, or Neutral? (Grades 5-8) 17

WATER

Fish and Food Webs (Grades 5-6) 18

The Efficiency of Fishing (Grades 5-8) 21

Purple Loosestrife & Wetlands (Grades 6-7) 23

Testing for Contaminants (Grades 6-8)........................... 25

Local Water Treatment (Grades 7-8) 27

Building Dams (Grades 7-8) 29

LAND

Erosion (Grades 5-6) 32

Tree Planting (Grades 5-8) 34

My Patchy Forest (Grades 6-8) 35

How Do Trees Clean the Air? (Grades 6-8) 37

Fretting Over Fertilizer (Grades 6-8) 38

Effects of Recreational Vehicles on the Environment (Grades 7-8)................... 40

My Corn (Grades 7-8) 42

The Urban Sprawl (Grades 7-8) 45

The Genetically Modified Organisms Debate (Grades 7-8) 47

POLLUTION AND ENERGY USE

Does Recycling Really Help? (Grades 5-7) 48

The Greenhouse Effect Game (Grades 5-8) 50

Classroom Composter (Grades 5-8) 52

Alternate Transportation Challenge (Grades 5-8) 54

Packaging Problems (Grades 5-8) 55

Battery Battle (Grades 5-8) 57

Table of Contents

Clearing the Air (Grades 5-8) 59
Car Craze (Grades 6-8) 60
Are You Energy and Water Efficient? (Grades 6-8) 62
Energy Trade-off (Grades 6-8) 64
Understanding Nuclear Energy (Grades 7-8) 66
Industrial Pollution (Grades 7-8) 68

INVASIVE SPECIES
Improving the Image (Grades 5-6) 69
Why Are Invasive Species so Invasive? (Grades 5-8) 70
Dealing with Invasive Species (Grades 5-8) 72
The Zebra Mussel Problem (Grades 7-8) 73

ENDANGERED OR EXTINCT ANIMALS AND PLANTS
Endangered Animal Encyclopedia (Grades 5-6) 74
Sea Turtle Conservation (Grades 5-6) 75
North American Endangered Animals (Grades 5-6) 77
Rainforest Simulation (Grades 5-6) 79
Species Identification (Grades 5-8) 81
Protecting the World's Animals (Grades 6-8) 83
Antibiotic Resistance (Grades 7-8) 85

CONCLUSION
Does the Government Care? (Grades 5-8) 87
Projecting into the Future (Grades 5-8) 88
Money Madness (Grades 6-8) 89
Conclusion 90

Answer Key 91

Teacher Assessment Rubric

Student's Name: _____

Criteria	Level 1	Level 2	Level 3	Level 4	Level
Understanding Concepts					
Demonstrates understanding of how humans have different effects on the environment	Little understanding	Some understanding	Good understanding	Excellent understanding	
Appreciates the importance of protecting the environment	Little appreciation	Some appreciation	Good appreciation	Excellent appreciation	
Demonstrates understanding of energy usage and waste	Little understanding	Some understanding	Good understanding	Excellent understanding	
Inquiry, design, and communication skills					
Demonstrates observation skills, and describes observations in written and drawn forms	Little evidence of observation skills	Some evidence of observation skills	Good evidence of observation skills	Excellent evidence of observation skills	
Applies observations to the making of conclusions appropriately	Conclusions reached have little basis in observations	Conclusions reached have some basis in observations	Conclusions reached have good basis in observations	Conclusions reached have strong basis in observations	
Demonstrates innovation in problem-solving	Little evidence of innovation	Some evidence of innovation	Good evidence of innovation	Excellent evidence of innovation	
Demonstrates creativity in communicating in written and drawn forms	Little evidence of creativity	Some evidence of creativity	Good evidence of creativity	Excellent evidence of creativity	
Relating science and technology to each other and the world outside of school					
Competency in the identification and use of parts of speech and other functions of written language	Little competency	Some competency	Satisfactory competency	Excellent competency	
Capacity to distinguish opinion from fact	Little capacity	Some capacity	Satisfactory capacity	Excellent capacity	

Student Self-Assessment Rubric

Name: _____   Date: _____

Put a check mark ✓ in the box that best describes your performance, then add your points to determine your score.

Expectations	My Performance				
	Needs Improvement (1 point)	Sometimes (2 points)	Frequently (3 points)	Almost Always (4 points)	Points
✓ I was focused and stayed on task.					
✓ My answers are thoughtful and show consistent effort.					
✓ I recorded accurately and in detail the procedures of experiments and my observations.					
✓ I proofread my work for spelling, grammar, and overall clarity.					
✓ I used my knowledge and experience to make connections between the environment and the world.					
✓ I can talk about and describe what I learned about the environment.					
✓ I know what I am good at.					
✓ I know what I need to work on.					
✓ I can use the resources available to me to research environmental issues and find answers.					

How We Impact the Environment

Introduction

The activities in this book have two objectives:

1. To teach students about human impacts on the environment.
2. To teach general science through the theme of the environment.

Throughout the activities research is required to find the answers to many questions. The necessary research can be done using any resources available:

- the Internet
- the library
- newspapers
- magazines

It is important to be able to distinguish between true and accurate information and false information. To ensure the information you find is true and accurate make sure that your reference:

- has a visible author name
- has been published by a publisher
- does not contain any points of view or bias
- refers to other resources (nobody knows everything)
- is current
- makes sense

The activities in this book fall under six topics:

- Introduction to Human Impacts on the Environment
- Water
- Land
- Pollution and Energy Use
- Invasive Species
- Endangered or Extinct Animals and Plants

Many of the activities in this book have open-ended questions that could have many different answers. Some answers have been provided in the answer key; however, these are not the only answers possible to the questions. These questions are designed to incite conversation and discussion.

Materials List

The students can perform the activities individually or in teams.

Each individual/team will need:

Consumables:

- bristol board
- string
- regular straws
- milk shake straws
- 1 plastic pop bottle with cap
- 1 cup (250 ml) of activated carbon pellets
- ½ cup (125 ml) of large gravel
- ½ cup (125 ml) of small gravel
- 3-4 cotton balls
- ½ cup (125 ml) of dirt
- ¼ cup (62.5 ml) of oil
- clay or Plasticine
- ¼ cup (62.5 ml) of confetti (bits of small paper)
- toothpicks
- popsicle sticks
- tape (duct, masking and clear)
- 3 potted plants of the same kind
- newspaper
- dirt
- peat moss
- calcium carbonate (or crushed egg shells)
- punch holes and black pepper
- balloon

Non-Consumables:

- scissors
- glue stick
- hole punch
- paperclips
- spoons
- 2 Dixie cups
- pieces of styrofoam
- metal washers
- large bowl
- safety goggles
- 3 glass beakers
- 5 pipettes
- 6 test tubes
- 1 test tube holder
- 1 large plastic cup
- sand
- 1 large water basin
- small stones
- ice cubes or plastic ice cubes
- buckets
- calculator (optional)
- ruler
- play money
- 6 bins or garbage bags
- 1 lb (454 g) of red wriggler worms
- 1 large bin with cover
- packaged products
- wire coat hanger
- plastic grocery bag
- dominos
- wheel pasta
- kidney beans
- sticky magnets
- safety pins
- 3 dice
- 100 ping-pong balls
- various small objects representing insects (the more the better, e.g., paperclips, pennies, metal washers, buttons, dimes, nickels, small beads, large beads, jelly beans, cheerios, thumb tacks, elastic bands)
- hula hoops
- rope
- yard or meter stick

In addition, you will need (one per class):

Consumables:

- ⮑ pesticide
- ⮑ 2 kinds of fertilizer
- ⮑ juvenile trees

Non-Consumables:

- ⮑ a watering jug (with a sprinkler spout)
- ⮑ universal indicator
- ⮑ bromothymol blue
- ⮑ stopwatch
- ⮑ garden spades or shovels
- ⮑ shoebox
- ⮑ blankets
- ⮑ sheets
- ⮑ nail and hammer
- ⮑ scale
- ⮑ plastic tube (fluorescent light tube packaging or equivalent)
- ⮑ electric blow dryer

What Impact Are We Having?

Objective:
- ➲ Learn about the impact people are having on the environment.
- ➲ Find out how aware people are about their environment.
- ➲ Learn to analyze surveys to obtain the information you need.

Introduction: Look around you! Almost everywhere you look something natural has been changed by people. Depending where you live you will see a different amount of change to the environment. In a rural town you will see roads, houses, farms, and fields, while in cities you will see sky scrapers, city buses, sidewalks, factories, and street lights. No matter where we live people are having an impact on their world. Is this a bad thing? A good thing? Let's find out!

Procedure:

Answer the following questions.

1. Name some of the impacts people are having on the environment.

   _____

   _____

   _____

2. How do you think people can reduce the impact they are having on their environment?

   _____

   _____

   _____

3. Do you think people can undo the effect they have already had on the environment?

   _____

   _____

   _____

4. Do you know of any measures that are in place in your town or city to help the environment?

   _____

   _____

   _____

5. Do you think the average person is more or less aware of their effect on the environment today than they were three years ago? Why?

   _____

   _____

   _____

Create and use a survey to find out what your friends, family, and neighbors think about human impacts on the environment. The purpose of a survey is not to see what one person thinks but to combine the information you collect to see what people in general are thinking. Use some or all of the following questions in your survey, or create your own ideas of human impacts on the environment.

Survey: Human Impacts on the Environment

Put a checkmark ✓ in the box beside your answer or record your answer on the lines provided.

1. Do you:
   - ☐ walk to work or school?
   - ☐ drive to work or school?
   - ☐ take the bus to work or school?
   - ☐ bike to work or school?
   - ☐ carpool to work or school?
   - ☐ other _____

2. What effect do you think you are having on the environment?
   - ☐ a very big impact
   - ☐ a big impact
   - ☐ an average impact
   - ☐ a small impact
   - ☐ no impact

3. Do you recycle?
   - ☐ yes
   - ☐ no

4. Do you compost?
   - ☐ yes
   - ☐ no

5. Name three negative impacts you think people are having on the environment.

   _____

   _____

   _____

6. Name three positive impacts you think people are having on the environment.

   _____

   _____

   _____

7. Do you think people need to change the way they treat the Earth?
   - ☐ yes
   - ☐ no

8. What type of vehicle do you drive on a daily basis?
   ☐ car or minivan
   ☐ motorcycle
   ☐ SUV or light truck
   ☐ Hummer
   ☐ Smart car
   ☐ bicycle
   ☐ other _____

9. Do you use florescent bulbs in your home. (bulbs that are shaped like a coil)?
   ☐ yes
   ☐ no

10. When you brush your teeth do you:
    ☐ let the water run?
    ☐ turn the water off while brushing?

11. How many large bags of garbage, on average, do you think you throw out each week?
    ☐ Less than 1
    ☐ 1
    ☐ 2
    ☐ 3
    ☐ 4 or more

12. Have you seen *An Inconvenient Truth* by Al Gore?
    ☐ yes
    ☐ no

13. Do you believe that global warming/climate change is a problem?
    ☐ yes
    ☐ no

14. What are three common sources of air pollutants?

    _____
    _____
    _____

15. In your opinion, how do you think people can reduce their effects on the environment?

    _____
    _____
    _____

➲ **Collect all the surveys** you hand out, and analyze them following the method on the next page.

What Impact Are We Having?

Data Analysis:

1. Use the table below or create your own. If you are familiar with Excel you may want to use it for a faster analysis.
2. Count how many people responded to each answer of the question.
3. For open questions, fill in the answers given and note how many people gave the same answer. You should also make note of whether the answer is correct or not, if there is a right answer.
4. Once you have all the answers in the table, circle or highlight the most common answers. Are they the most common answers for everyone in the class? Why?
5. Do you think people in your community think they are having a big impact on their environment?
6. Make notes about why you think people answered the way they did. Why might people answer incorrectly? What does this mean for the environment? How can this problem be fixed?

Question	A	B	C	D	Comments
1.					
2.					
3.					
4.					
5.					
6.					
7.					
8.					
9.					
10.					
11.					
12.					
13.					
14.					
15.					

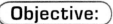

Environmental Dictionary

Objective: ➲ Learn the vocabulary of an environmentalist.

Introduction: There are a lot of big words used to explain the effects we are having on the environment and it is important to know what they all mean. Some of these words include:

- ➲ acid rain
- ➲ biodiversity
- ➲ carcinogen
- ➲ climate change
- ➲ contamination
- ➲ deforestation
- ➲ desalination
- ➲ ecological footprint

- ➲ ecosystem
- ➲ extinction
- ➲ global warming
- ➲ indigenous species
- ➲ invasive species
- ➲ ozone
- ➲ renewable resources
- ➲ sustainability

Procedure:

1. Make an environmental dictionary using the above words and others that you might come across. Add at least one word each week and include its definition, an example, and an image. You can use the following example or come up with your own.

Invasive Species – a plant or animal that has been introduced to an area, where it could not have appeared on its own, from a different area.

Example: The zebra mussel was introduced to North America from Europe. It has no natural predators here. It can reproduce extremely fast and cause many problems.

2. At the end of the year create questions for a Jeopardy style game using the vocabulary you have learned. For the rules of Jeopardy see http://en.wikipedia.org/wiki/Jeopardy.

Ecological Footprint

Objective: ➲ Learn about ecological footprints and how to reduce yours.

Introduction: What is a footprint? It is the imprint you leave on the earth as you walk around. What is an ecological footprint? It is the imprint you leave on the environment as you live your life. The more water, electricity, living space, and food resources you use, the larger your ecological footprint.

Procedure: Use the following quiz to find out your ecological footprint.

1. How old are you?
   - ☐ a. 10 years old or younger
   - ☐ b. 11-15 years old
   - ☐ c. 16-20 years old
   - ☐ d. 21-25 years old
   - ☐ e. 26 years old or older

2. How many people live in your town/city?
   - ☐ a. Less than 1000 (small town)
   - ☐ b. 1001-10,000 (average town)
   - ☐ c. 10,001-100,000 (big town)
   - ☐ d. 100,001 – 1,000,000 (city)
   - ☐ e. 1,000,000 or more (metropolitan)

3. How often do you eat meat?
   - ☐ a. None – I'm vegan (no animal products)
   - ☐ b. None – I'm vegetarian (no meat)
   - ☐ c. Once or twice a week
   - ☐ d. Everyday
   - ☐ e. In almost every meal

4. How much of the food you eat is processed (non-natural and packaged)?
   - ☐ a. Almost none
   - ☐ b. One quarter (25%)
   - ☐ c. Half
   - ☐ d. Three-quarters (75%)
   - ☐ e. Most

5. How much garbage do you throw out?
   - ☐ a. Less than 1 garbage bag per week
   - ☐ b. 1 garbage bag per week
   - ☐ c. 2 garbage bags per week
   - ☐ d. 3 garbage bags per week
   - ☐ e. 4 or more garbage bags per week

6. How many people live in your home?
   - ☐ a. 2
   - ☐ b. 3
   - ☐ c. 4
   - ☐ d. 5
   - ☐ e. 6 or more

7. What kind of home do you live in?
   - ☐ a. Apartment Building (4 or more floors)
   - ☐ b. Apartment Building (3 floors or less)
   - ☐ c. Row house (4 or 5 homes attached together side-by-side)
   - ☐ d. House
   - ☐ e. Mansion

8. How much time do you spend on a bus to get to school?
   - ☐ a. 0 minutes
   - ☐ b. 1-20 minutes
   - ☐ c. 21-40 minutes
   - ☐ d. 41-60 minutes
   - ☐ e. more than 60 minutes

9. How much time do you spend in a car to get to school?
   - ☐ a. 0 minutes
   - ☐ b. 1-20 minutes
   - ☐ c. 21-40 minutes
   - ☐ d. 41-40 minutes
   - ☐ e. more than 60 minutes

10. How many hours have you spent on a plane in the past year?
    - ☐ a. 0 hours
    - ☐ b. 1-3 hours
    - ☐ c. 4-10 hours
    - ☐ d. 11-25 hours
    - ☐ e. 26 or more hours

To add up your ecological footprint follow the point chart below:

a = 1 point   b = 2 points   c = 3 points   d = 4 points   e = 5 points

➲ If you have 11-20 points – You have a very small ecological footprint. If everyone lived like you we would not have an environmental problem.

➲ If you have 21-30 points – You have a small ecological footprint. If everyone lives like you we would need two planets.

➲ If you have 31-40 points – You have an average ecological footprint. If everyone lived like you we would need five planets.

➲ If you have 41-50 points – You have a large ecological footprint. If everyone lived like you we would need 15 planets.

➲ If you have 51-55 points – You have a very large ecological footprint. If everyone lived like you we would need 25 planets.

If you were to divide up all the habitable land on Earth among all the people on Earth, each person would have 4.4 acres (1.8 hectares) of land that they could use. This amount of land is the average ecological footprint people on our planet should have. The average ecological footprint for North America, however, is 23 acres (9.3 hectares), and if everyone lived like we did we would need 13 planets.

Positive, Negative, or Neutral

Objective: Learn how different impacts on the environment have different effects.

Procedure: For the following human impacts write down what type of impact (positive, neutral, or negative) it is and why.

An example is provided for you:

Deforestation: <u>negative, because trees that are cut down and used in factories can no longer</u> <u>create oxygen from carbon dioxide and they cannot provide shelter for plants and animals.</u>

Air pollution: _____

_____

Fishing: _____

_____

Land Use: _____

_____

Mining: _____

_____

Waste Treatment: _____

_____

Water Treatment: _____

_____

Recycling: _____

_____

Tree Planting: _____

_____

Hunting: _____

_____

Dredging for Oil: _____

_____

Fish and Food Webs

Objectives:
➲ Learn the difference between food chains and food webs.
➲ Create an in-class marine food web.

Introduction: Everything in nature is connected in some way, and these connections are almost always very complicated. You are going to examine the connections between different aquatic (water) creatures through the following games.

Materials:
➲ organism cards　　　➲ hole punch
➲ bristol board　　　➲ glue stick
➲ scissors　　　➲ string

Procedure:

1. Print out the following organism cards or make your own.
2. Cut the cards out and glue them to a piece of Bristol board that is the same size as the card.
3. Punch a hole in each of the two upper corners of the card and attach a piece of string long enough to go over your head.
4. Turn the cards face down on a table and mix them all up.
5. Take one card from the pile and, without looking at it, hang it around your neck so that the blank side of the card is lying against your back.

Game One

1. Everyone should have a card hanging against their back.
2. You now have to try and guess what organism you are by asking yes or no questions only.
3. Questions you might want to ask are:
   a. Do I eat fish?
   b. Am I near the bottom/top of the food chain?
   c. Am I eaten by bears?
4. Once you have figured out what you are put the card against your stomach so people can see what you are. Continue to answer questions for other people until everyone has figured out what they are.

Game Two

1. Everyone should stand in a circle.
2. One person, the teacher, will be the sun and stand in the middle of the circle.
3. The purpose of this game is to create the food web by connecting yourself, using string, with things you eat or that eat you.
4. Anything that gets its energy from the sun will be linked to the sun.
5. Go around the circle and have each person choose to create a link with one of the creatures they eat or are eaten by.
6. The sun should be in charge of handing out and cutting the string.
7. Make sure you hold on tight to your end of the string.
8. Continue going around the circle until everyone is connected.

Fish and Food Webs

9. Once everyone is connected, read the following scenarios out loud. If an organism will benefit from the outcome of the scenario, that person should raise the arm holding the strings into the air. If an organism is negatively affected by the outcome, that person should sit down.

Scenarios:

1. Global warming is causing the arctic ice to disappear and the polar bears can no longer hunt. All the polar bears die.

2. The migration of the caribou is disturbed due to oil drilling. All the caribou disappear.

3. Fishers fish out all the cod.

4. A new fish is introduced to the lake and it eats all the zooplankton.

5. An oil spill stops the birds from being able to fly and all the seals get really sick and can't hunt.

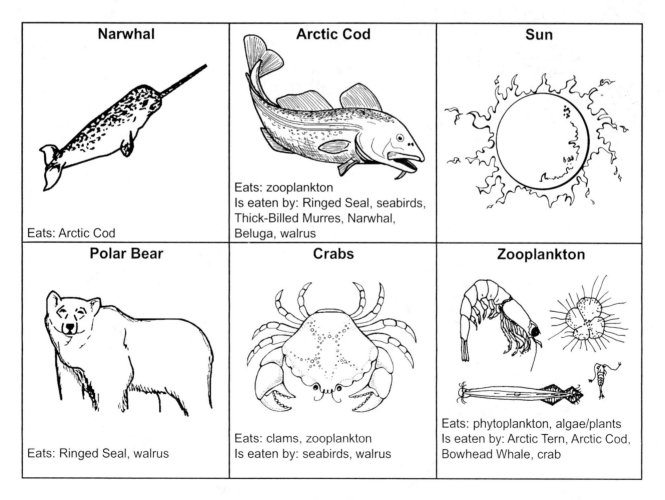

Narwhal	**Arctic Cod**	**Sun**
Eats: Arctic Cod	Eats: zooplankton Is eaten by: Ringed Seal, seabirds, Thick-Billed Murres, Narwhal, Beluga, walrus	
Polar Bear	**Crabs**	**Zooplankton**
Eats: Ringed Seal, walrus	Eats: clams, zooplankton Is eaten by: seabirds, walrus	Eats: phytoplankton, algae/plants Is eaten by: Arctic Tern, Arctic Cod, Bowhead Whale, crab

Phytoplankton

Gets its energy from the sun.
Is eaten by: zooplankton, insects

Algae and Plants

Get their energy from the sun.
Are eaten by: insects, caribou,
zooplankton

Seabirds

Eats: clams, Arctic Cod, insects,
crabs

Ringed Seal

Eats: Arctic Cod
Eaten by: Polar Bears

Insects

Eats: phytoplankton, algae, and plants
Are eaten by: Arctic Tern, seabirds

Walrus

Eats: Arctic Cod, clams, crab
Is eaten by: Polar Bears

Beluga Whale

Eats: Arctic Cod

Arctic Tern

Eats: insects, zooplankton

Bowhead Whale

Eats: zooplankton

Clams

Eats: zooplankton
Eaten by: crab, walrus, seabirds

Caribou

Eats: algae and plants

Thick-Billed Murres

Eats: Arctic Cod

The Efficiency of Fishing

Objectives:
➲ Learn about **sustainable** fishing.
➲ Play a simulation game to better understand the importance of efficient fishing.

Introduction:

What is a renewable resource? Are fish a renewable resource? They are only renewable if they are fished sustainably. This means that there has to be a limit to how many fish can be captured so that the populations can reproduce and create enough offspring to replace the fish caught. If fish are fished too heavily they will not be able to reproduce fast enough and may eventually die out. If fish are not fished enough people will go hungry because millions of people rely on fish as their primary source of food.

Fishers use different methods to catch fish: hook and line, nets, bottom trawlers, etc. Each of these methods has a different effect on the number of fish and other creatures that are caught. Let's explore these differences by playing a simulation game. At the end you will try to figure out how fishers can maximize their catch while keeping it sustainable.

➲ paperclips (hook)
➲ hole punch
➲ 1 ft (30 cm) length of string
➲ small pieces of styrofoam (fish)
➲ scissors
➲ metal washers (bottom feeding fish)
➲ spoons (trawlers)

➲ large bowl
➲ Dixie cups (nets)
➲ water
➲ one straw
➲ extra cups (or paper boats)
➲ duct tape

Procedure:

1. Punch holes in the pieces of styrofoam. Use the punched holes as small fish and the punched styrofoam as large fish.
2. Pour all the styrofoam and washers into the large bowl and mix.
3. Fill the bowl ¾ full with water.
4. Unbend a paperclip so that it forms a hook. Attached one end of your string to your hook. This is your hook and line.
5. Punch one hole along the rim of your cup and insert one end of the straw into the hole. Bend the straw on the inside of the cup and use a piece of duct tape to tape it to the inside of the cup. Bend the side of the cup opposite from the hole so that it lies flat against your desk. This is your net.

The Efficiency of Fishing

6. Your spoon is your bottom trawler.
7. In a group of four, sit around the bowl of "fish".
8. Have one person be the time keeper
9. Taking turns, see how long it takes to collect 20 fish using the hook and line.
   Replace the fish in the bowl after each turn.
10. Record your time and the number of each type of fish you caught.
11. See how long it takes to collect 20 fish using the bottom trawler (spoon).
    Replace the fish in the bowl after each turn.
12. Record your time and the number of each type of fish you caught.
13. See how long it takes to collect 20 fish using the net (cup and straw).
    Replace the fish in the bowl after each turn.
14. Record your time and the number of each type of fish you caught.
15. Examine your results.
    a. Which type of fishing was the fastest?
    b. Which type of fishing caught the most large fish? Small fish? Bottom feeders?

Compare your results with the rest of your group and class and discuss. Which type of fishing do you think is most sustainable? Why?

Type of Fishing	Time and Fish Caught			
	Time to catch 20 fish (seconds)	Number of large fish (punched styrofoam)	Number of small fish (punched styrofoam holes)	Number of bottom feeders (metal washers)
Hook and Line (paperclips and string)				
Net (cup and straw)				
Bottom Trawler (spoon)				

Purple Loosestrife and Wetlands

Objective:

➲ Learn about invasive species and the vulnerability of wetlands.

Introduction:

Have you ever wondered how water is filtered by nature? Humans have invented ways to clean water after it has been used, but before we were around how did nature recycle its water? Nature uses wetlands to filter water, but how? It works in much the same way as our own water treatment plants (see "Local Water Treatment" on page 27). Wetlands are very important for the balance of nature, but there are serious threats to these important ecosystems.

Procedure:

Using the resources available to help you, find the answer to the following questions.

1. Give a definition of a wetland.

_____

_____

_____

2. Give three examples of types of wetlands and explain the differences.

_____

_____

_____

3. Give three examples of native animals that live in or around wetlands.

_____

_____

_____

4. What is the closest wetland to your school?

_____

_____

_____

5. Where did purple loosestrife come from?

_____

_____

Purple Loosestrife and Wetlands

6. How did purple loosestrife get introduced to North America?

    _____

    _____

    _____

7. What effect is purple loosestrife having on the North American environment?

    _____

    _____

    _____

    _____

8. Give two reasons why purple loosestrife is so hard to get rid of.

    _____

    _____

9. How many seeds can one purple loosestrife plant produce in a year?

    _____

10. How are people controlling the spread of purple loosestrife?

    _____

    _____

    _____

    _____

11. Are there any other plants or animals that are threatening wetlands?

    _____

    _____

    _____

Testing for Contaminants

Objective: ⊃ Learn how to find out if water is safe to drink using simple chemistry.

Introduction:

When you drink water, how do you know if it's clean? Does it look clean? Does it smell clean? Does that mean that it is actually clean? Some water has invisible contaminants that could make you sick. The water that comes out of a tap or water fountain has been cleaned, but water from lakes or rivers has not, so how do you know when water is safe to drink? Many times you can't test the water so if you are hiking or camping and need to drink water you can use a water filter or water purification tablets to make the water safe.

In this activity we are going to see what tests we can use to see if water is contaminated or not. In order to do this we use chemistry.

Equipment:

⊃ safety goggles (for each student)
⊃ three beakers of unlabeled water samples, labeled 1, 2 and 3 (one contaminated with pesticides, one contaminated with fertilizer, and one of tap water)
⊃ one pipette for each beaker
⊃ six empty test tubes per group
⊃ universal indicator with pipette
⊃ bromothymol blue with pipette
⊃ one test tube holder per group
⊃ one handout per group

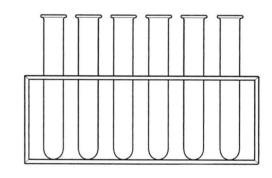

Procedure:

1. Label your test tubes 1a, 1b, 2a, 2b, 3a, 3b.
2. Add 10 drops of water from the first beaker into test tubes 1a and 1b.
3. Add 10 drops of water from the second beaker into test tubes 2a and 2b.
4. Add 10 drops of water from the third beaker into test tubes 3a and 3b.
5. Note any water discoloration or smell in your table.
6. Add 1 drop of bromothymol blue to test tubes 1a, 2a, and 3a.
7. Add 1 drop of universal indicator to test tubes 1b, 2b, and 3b.
8. Observe any color changes in your test tubes in your table.

Observation Sheet: Testing for Contaminants

Water Sample	Bromothymol Blue		Universal Indicator	
	Test tube	Observation	Test tube	Observation
Beaker 1	1a		1b	
Beaker 2	2a		2b	
Beaker 3	3a		3b	

Extension:

1. Why did you test the water with two different chemicals?

   _____

   _____

   _____

2. What did you notice about the color change?

   _____

   _____

   _____

3. Which beaker(s) do you think were contaminated? Why do you think this?

   _____

   _____

   _____

4. Which beaker was filled with regular tap water? Why do you think this?

   _____

   _____

   _____

5. Why do you think the color of the water changed?

   _____

   _____

   _____

6. Compare your results with your classmates. Are the results the same? Why or why not?

   _____

   _____

   _____

Local Water Treatment

Objective: ➲ Learn how water is recycled by creating your own water filtration system.

Introduction:

We use water every day and we use a lot of it. The water we use is usually clean and drinkable, but when we are done with it, it is often dirty and contaminated. How is it that we never run out of clean water? We recycle it. But how do you recycle water?

Water is essential for life and we need clean water to drink so that we don't get sick. The water that comes out of your taps at home and school is clean water that has been recycled. Dirty water that has been used goes down the drain, into the sewers, and gets collected at a water treatment plant. Then what happens?

Using what you know about water and your imagination, explain what you think is happening in each step of this diagram. Start with the water that goes down the drain and finish with the water that comes out of the tap.

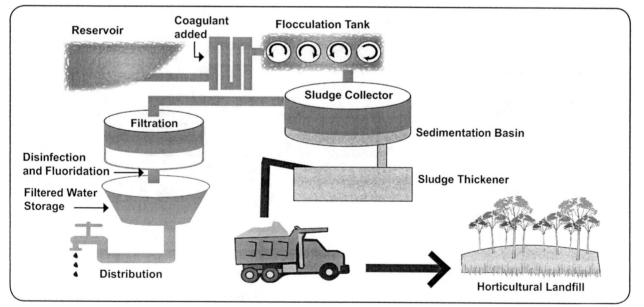

Making a Water Filtration System: You can make your very own water recycling plant for your home or classroom.

Materials:
- ➲ one 68 fluid ounce (2 liter) plastic pop bottle with cap
- ➲ large plastic cup that will hold the pop bottle upside down
- ➲ 3 to 4 cotton balls
- ➲ ½ cup (125 ml) of dirt
- ➲ 2 cups (500 ml) of sand
- ➲ ¼ cup (62.5 ml) of oil
- ➲ 1 cup (250 ml) of activated carbon pellets
- ➲ ¼ cup (62.5 ml) of confetti (bits of small paper)
- ➲ ½ cup (125 ml) of large gravel
- ➲ 2 cups (500 ml) of water
- ➲ ½ cup (125 ml) of small gravel
- ➲ scissors or box cutter

Making a Water Filtration System:

Procedure:

1. Use the box cutter to cut off the bottom of the bottle. Leave the cap on.
2. Turn the bottle over so that the cap is down and the big opening you just made is up and place it in the large plastic cup.
3. Put the cotton in first, pushing it down until it is stuck in the neck of the bottle.
4. Pour the large gravel in.
5. Pour the smaller gravel in.
6. Pour the sand in.
7. Pour the activated carbon in.
8. Mix the dirt, oil, and paper pieces with the water.
9. Remove the cap from the bottle.
10. Pour the dirty water into your water filter.
11. Watch what happens as the water passes through each layer of the filter.

Extension:

1. Did your filter clean the dirty water?

_____

_____

2. What would happen if you put the sand in first?

_____

_____

3. Why do you put cotton at the bottom?

_____

_____

4. What does the activated carbon do?

_____

_____

5. How long would it take to filter one gallon (four liters) of water using this system?

_____

_____

6. How does this compare to how your town/city recycles water?

_____

_____

Building Dams

Objective: ➲ Learn how dams can be used to create energy by creating your own.

Introduction:

People use all sorts of ways to create electricity. Can you think of four ways people can create electricity to power their homes? Hydroelectric dams are a common way to create vast amounts of electricity for use by cities and towns. But how do they work? How can water be turned into energy? Here you will get the chance to create your own dam and explore how one can be used to create power. Before starting, answer questions one to four of the handout.

Building a Dam:

Before you start building, look at pictures of real dams, like the Hoover Dam, to get an idea of how they might be built. Do human-made dams look anything like beaver dams? You should notice that wherever there is a dam there is one side with high water and another side with low water. The high side is the side the water is flowing from. The water is slowed down by the dam and forced through small openings where the water speeds up, making turbines turn. The turning action is turned into power that we can use as electricity.

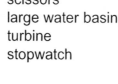

Equipment: (suggestion only)

➲ clay or Plasticine
➲ string (cut into 3 foot or 100 cm lengths
➲ popsicle sticks
➲ regular sized straws (axle of the turbine)
➲ toothpicks

➲ large milkshake straws (or equivalent plastic tubing)
➲ tape
➲ scissors
➲ large water basin, one per group
➲ turbine
➲ stopwatch

Procedure:

1. Use the diagram and any of the supplies provided to create your own dam. You will not be creating electricity from your dam but you can test how powerful your dam would be if it were real. You may need to test your dam several times to get it to work properly. Work in teams.

2. To test your dam poke a hole in the end of the straw (attached to your turbine) that is sticking out of your dam and tie a length of string to the straw. When you add the water to your dam, test how long it takes for the string to wind around the straw. The faster it winds the more efficient your dam would be at creating electricity.

Building Dams

3. Answer questions one to four before making your dam and question five after.

(**Extension:**)

1. Name four ways that electricity can be created.

   _____

   _____

   _____

   _____

2. What is a dam?

   _____

   _____

   _____

3. Why do beavers build dams?

   _____

   _____

   _____

4. How is a hydroelectric dam different from a beaver dam?

   _____

   _____

   _____

5. In the space provided draw a cross-section of your dam as it would appear in real life. Label all the parts.

Building Dams

6. In your opinion, is using dams to create electricity good or bad for the environment? Why?

_____

_____

_____

_____

7. How does the dam affect the environment around it?

_____

_____

_____

8. What consequences might this have for:

a) people _____

_____

_____

b) animals _____

_____

_____

c) plants _____

_____

_____

9. What do you think is the best way to power your home? Why?

_____

_____

_____

_____

_____

_____

_____

_____

Erosion

Objective: ➲ See how erosion works and discuss the ways it might affect the environment.

Introduction:

Imagine for a minute that you are building a sand castle. You have just finished putting the flag at the top when someone throws a bucket of water over your sand castle. What happens? Your sand castle gets destroyed, but how? As the water is flowing over the sand that you used to build your sand castle, it is carrying away little grains of sand. This is called erosion. Erosion is the downhill movement of something solid, like dirt, sand, or even rock by water, wind, or ice. Have you ever seen a snow-topped mountain that has big crevices down the sides? These crevices are pathways created by years and years of water flowing down the mountain from the melting snow. Let's see how erosion works.

Equipment:
➲ a large pile of sand
➲ a pile of small stones
➲ a watering jug (with a sprinkler spout)
➲ large basin (for building your mountain in)
➲ ice cubes or plastic ice cubes

Procedure:

1. Divide the class into four groups. Each group will work together to build a mountain.

2. In your large basin you are going to build a mountain using stones and sand. Start by building a pyramid of stones. Make sure that your mountain doesn't touch the sides of the basin. Next cover your stones with sand. You can make the mountain look any way you like. The sand doesn't have to cover all the stones, some mountains are rocky, but if you want to make a smooth mountain you can do that, too. Use some water to pack your mountain like you would a sand castle.

3. Once you have built your mountain use the following scenarios to make predictions about what you think will happen to the mountain. Write and draw your predictions in the table on page 33. Don't do anything else to your mountain until you have made all your predictions.

   a. Water falls on your mountain from above.
   b. Water hits your mountain at its base (like ocean waves washing against the shore)
   c. Wind blows against your mountain from one side.
   d. A piece of ice at the top of your mountain breaks off and slides down the side.

4. Once you have written down your prediction, each group will test one prediction and everyone will observe what happens. Write down and draw your observations in the table provided. You can test each of the above in the following ways:

   a. Gently pour water from the watering can directly over your mountain.
   b. Pour water into the basin without letting the stream of water hit the mountain.

Erosion

   c. Blow hard against the side of your mountain. Have three students blow at the same time for the best effect.

   d. Place an ice cube near the top of your mountain. Keep adding ice cubes until they start to slide down the side.

5. Once the table has been filled in, answer the questions below.

Situation	Prediction	Observation
a. Water over top		
b. Water against base		
c. Wind		
d. Ice		

6. Did any of the observations surprise you? Why or why not? _____
_____

7. Where else can erosion happen, besides on mountains? _____
_____

8. Erosion is important for the environment. Why? _____
_____

9. Erosion can be bad for the environment. How? _____
_____

10. Why?_____

Tree Planting

Objective:

⊃ Reduce your ecological footprint by planting trees in your community.

Introduction:

There are a lot of reasons why you would want to plant trees. Trees are very important for the planet. They help clean the air by changing carbon dioxide into oxygen; they are used for food and as homes by many animals, birds, and insects; they create shade which can protect people from the sun; and they provide nutrients to the soil and prevent erosion. Planting trees is also a good way to replace trees that have been cut down for wood, fuel, or agriculture.

As a class, decide on a place in your community where you think trees should be planted. Is there a park without enough shade? Could your school yard use more trees?

Once you have found a spot to plant your trees discuss the following questions:

⊃ Is tree planting a positive, neutral, or negative human impact? Why?
⊃ What kind(s) of trees should you plant in your area? Why?
⊃ Should you plant more than one kind of tree? Why?
⊃ How should the trees be planted? In rows? In a circle? Randomly? Why?

Equipment:

⊃ trees – these can be purchased or ordered from your local nursery
⊃ garden spades or shovels
⊃ buckets
⊃ water

Here are some things you should consider when planning your own tree planting project:

⊃ Order your trees so that they arrive very close to the planting date. Trees should be planted within two days. Choose trees that are hardy and that can grow in harsh conditions. Make sure the trees you choose are able to survive the climate in your area.
⊃ When you order your trees ask if your trees need any special planting treatment such as peat or ash.
⊃ Keep a space of at least 8 feet (2.4 meters) between trees.
⊃ Plant your trees in the late spring to give the trees time to grow and become strong before winter.

For more information about tree planting, visit

http://www.seedlingnursery.com/downloads/PLNGTRPL.PDF

My Patchy Forest

Objective: ➲ Learn how the way forests are clear-cut affects their health and growth.

Introduction:

A forest is being used to harvest wood. The lumber people don't want to cut down the whole forest. They want to cut as much wood as possible without killing the forest. They want your help.

Procedure:

1. Look at the following clear-cutting shapes. Predict which one will give the most wood and the least damage to the forest as a whole. Write your prediction in the space provided.
2. Cut out the shapes and trace them onto a piece of grid paper.
3. Count the number of squares (area) within the outline. Only count full squares.
4. Measure the length of the outline (perimeter) using the grid paper squares as guidelines or a ruler. Use the perimeter formula for a triangle to get a more exact measurement without a ruler.
5. Write your measurements in the space provided.

Extension:

1. Using the following clues, decide which of the shapes would be best for the lumber people:

   a. The more trees the lumber people can cut down, the better for the company.

   _____
   _____
   _____

   b. The more edge a forest has the more animals are at risk. (Why?)

   _____
   _____
   _____

2. Can you think of an even better shape (or shapes) the lumber people could use?

   _____
   _____
   _____

Shape	Prediction	Area	Perimeter	Decision
Square				
Circle				
Stripes				
Irregular				
Cross				

My Patchy Forest

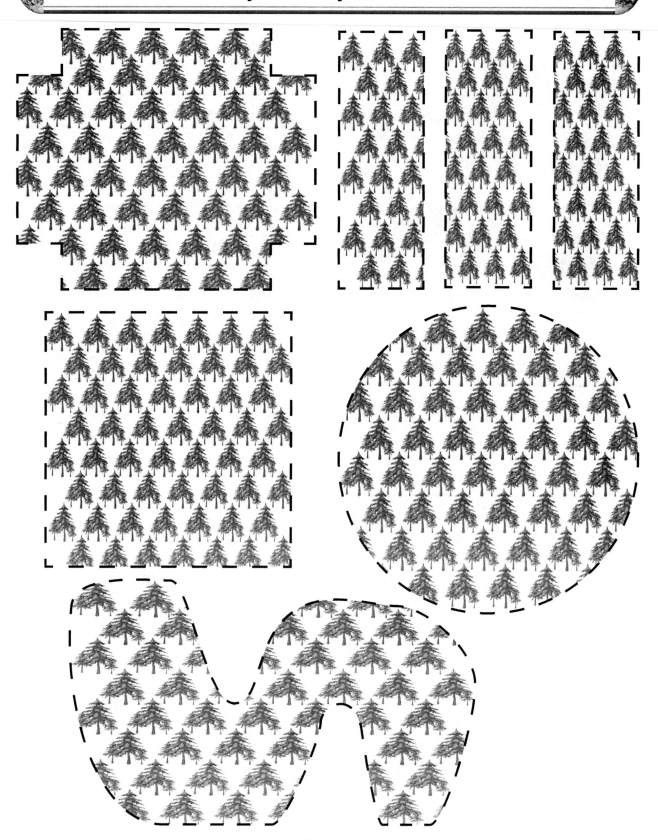

How Do Trees Clean the Air?

Objectives:
- ➲ Learn how trees clean the air.
- ➲ Calculate how many trees are needed to clean the air.

Equipment:
- ➲ calculator

Procedure: According to scientists it takes 1,000 trees to replace 4,375 lbs (20,000 kg) of carbon dioxide with oxygen.

A. Estimate answers to the following questions. If you don't know, use the averages provided in parentheses. Note: 1 gallon of gas releases 20 pounds of carbon dioxide (or 1 liter of gas releases 2.36 kg of carbon dioxide).

1. How many miles/kilometers does your family car travel in one year? (12,500 mi ; 20,000 km)

   _____

2. How many gallons/liters does your car use to travel that distance? (29 mi/gal ; 12 km/L)

   _____

3. How much carbon dioxide is released by your car to travel that distance?

   _____

4. How many trees would it take to use up all that carbon dioxide produced?

   _____

5. What is the population of your city/town?

   _____

6. If 1 in 6 people in your city/town have a car, how many trees would you need to plant to use up all the carbon dioxide produced by everyone in your town per year?

   _____

B. Try calculating how many trees you would need to plant to use up the carbon dioxide created by:

1. a plane traveling from New York to Paris (0.2 mi/gal ; 0.08 km/L).

   _____

2. a motorcycle traveling 12.4 mi/20 km every day for one year (43 mi/gal ; 18 km/L).

   _____

3. a freight train traveling from Denver to Houston (1.1 mi/gal ; 0.47 km/L).

   _____

4. a bus traveling from Chicago to Orlando (6 mi/gal ; 2.6 km/L).

   _____

Fretting Over Fertilizer

Objectives:
- Learn what fertilizer is and how it's used.
- Discover ways to manage fertilizer run-off and disposal.
- Experiment with fertilizers.

Equipment:
- 3 potted plants of the same kind per group
- 2 different kinds of fertilizer (purchased from local nursery)
- a sunlit area
- water
- ruler

Procedure One:

1. Fill in the steps of the fertilizer cycle in the following diagram.

2. Circle the biggest problem with this fertilizer cycle. Why is it a problem?

   a. Grass is eaten by a cow, the cow defecates, fertilizer goes into the ground and is absorbed by grass which is eaten by the cow.
   b. Fertilizer is also used on crops, goes into the soil and is absorbed, making the plants grow faster.
   c. The fertilizer in the ground also leaches out and into the water.

3. What is fertilizer?

   _____

   _____

4. How does fertilizer make plants grow faster?

   _____

   _____

   _____

5. What happens if the cows produce more fertilizer than the farmer can use on his/her crops?

   _____

   _____

6. If you had a cow and it was producing more fertilizer than you could use in your garden, what would you do with it?

   _____

   _____

7. What happens if there is too much fertilizer? Why?

   _____

   _____

   _____

Fretting Over Fertilizer

Procedure Two:

1. Label your plants A, B, and C.
2. Label your fertilizers A and B.
3. Add the same amount of fertilizer to each plant following the directions on the bag or bottle. Plant C doesn't get a fertilizer.
4. Make sure that all your plants are close together and have plenty of sunlight.
5. Rotate your plants clockwise one spot every week. Why?
6. Fertilize your plants every week. Make sure each plant gets the same amount of fertilizer and water and that it's the same amount every week.
7. Measure your plants on the same day every week for 6 weeks.
8. Measure from the dirt to the base of the highest leaf.
9. Fill in the following table:

Week	PLANT A			PLANT B			PLANT C		
	Height	Position	Fertilizer and Water	Height	Position	Fertilizer and Water	Height	Position	Fertilizer and Water
0									
1									
2									
3									
4									
5									

Extension:

1. Why did only two of the plants get fertilizer? _____
2. Why did you rotate your plants every week? _____
3. Why did you keep the amount of fertilizer and water the same? _____
4. What did you observe from your experiment? _____
5. Which plant grew the most? _____
6. Which plant grew the least? _____
7. Which plant grew the fastest? _____
8. Which plant grew the slowest? _____
9. Combine your data with the other groups. Which fertilizer was the best? _____
10. Did the fertilized plants grow faster than the plant without fertilizer? _____

Effects of Recreational Vehicles on the Environment

Objectives:
- ➲ Understand the importance of environmental stewardship.
- ➲ Learn how to have fun and protect the environment.

Procedure:
1. Examine the two images below.
2. On a separate sheet write down what environmental effects you think the All Terrain Vehicle (ATV) or motor boat would have if they followed the trails. Include ideas to protect the environment.

ATVing Through the Woods

Motor Boating on a Sunny Day

Effects of Recreational Vehicles on the Environment

Extension:

Fill in the table below. Compare your answers with a partner.

Recreational Vehicle	Why it's fun	What harm it can do to the environment	How to have fun and help the environment
All Terrain Vehicles			
Speed Boats			
Dirt Bikes			
Snowmobiles			
Sea-Doos			

My Corn

Objectives:
- ➲ Play a game to observe the ways people share within a community.
- ➲ Use what you learned about sharing to explain what is happening in agriculture and many big companies.

Equipment:
- ➲ box with a lid, with a flap cut into the top big enough to put your hand in (one for each group)
- ➲ play money ($50 per student)

Procedure:

1. Split the class into two groups. Have one person be the moderator in each group. Each group will be playing the game separately.

2. Give each person $50 in small bills ($1, $5, $10).

3. The setting for the game is as follows:

   You are a community of farmers. Each of you has your own farm. Every week (or every turn) whatever money the community makes as a unit gets multiplied by two and divided equally among the resident farmers. The money the community makes is based on the farmers and what they are willing to share with the community. For each turn the box will be passed around and each farmer can put as little or as much money in the box as they want. Everyone else must close their eyes so they cannot see how much has been put in the box. If you do not want to put any money in, you do not have to.

4. Once everyone has had a turn the money is counted, multiplied by two, and divided equally among the students.

5. Repeat this process ten times, keeping track of the total money (before multiplying by two) after each turn.

6. After ten turns, discuss, as a community, what trends were observed. How much money did you make as a community? Who has the most money? Why? Who has the least money? Why? What do you think would have happened if the game had continued another 10 turns?

7. Compare your community results with the other team. Are they the same? Why or why not?

My Corn

Extension:

1. In this game, farmers are able to contribute what they want to the community. The more each person contributes, the better off everyone will be.

   What is the most money each person could have at the end of 10 weeks? Why does no one have this much?

   _____

   _____

   _____

2. Now, imagine that the community produces corn. This community is "owned" by a big company that has created a type of corn that is resistant to pests, produces sweet, juicy corn, and doesn't produce seeds. Farmers can make a lot of money selling this corn, but they have to keep buying the seeds from the company.

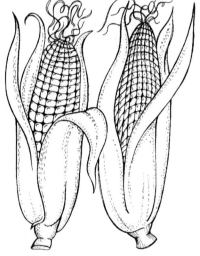

3. What would have happened in your game if, instead of dividing the money equally among all the farmers, 25% is given to this company to buy seeds? Try it.

4. How much less would each farmer make?

   _____

5. How much would the company make?

   _____

6. What are the environmental risks of using this type of agriculture?

   _____

   _____

   _____

7. Is there a better way? What could it be?

   _____

   _____

   _____

My Corn

Week	Total = Money Made by the Community	Community Growth = Total x 2	Personal Growth = Community Growth/Number of Farmers
Week 1			
Week 2			
Week 3			
Week 4			
Week 5			
Week 6			
Week 7			
Week 8			
Week 9			
Week 10			
Total			

Week	Total	Community Growth	Personal Growth	75% of Community Growth (x)	x/Number of Farmers	Company Profit = 25% of Community Growth
Week 1						
Week 2						
Week 3						
Week 4						
Week 5						
Week 6						
Week 7						
Week 8						
Week 9						
Week 10						
Total						

The Urban Sprawl

Objectives: ➲ Learn how urban sprawl is becoming a big problem in cities.

Introduction:

Imagine a city. In the middle of the city you have a lot of apartment buildings and office buildings. Around the middle of the city you have a lot of townhouses, single homes that are very close together, strip malls, and small businesses. Just outside the city you have the "suburbs", a suburban community where the homes have some land and the neighborhood is family-friendly. With all these "layers" of homes within a city, the city itself gets spread out (or sprawled) over a much larger distance than what you would consider "downtown".

This urban sprawl is having an important effect on our environment, but how and why? Using the following information you will create a map and find out just what is happening.

Population Information for the City of Sprawlville

Distance from the center of Sprawlville	Number of people
5 miles/km	200,000
10 miles/km	400,000
15 miles/km	600,000
20 miles/km	725,000
25 miles/km	800,000
30 miles/km	850,000
35 miles/km	900,000
40 miles/km	950,000
45 miles/km	975,000
50 miles/km	1,000,000

The Urban Sprawl

Procedure:

1. Using the above information, draw a graph in the space provided. Put the distance along the bottom of your graph and the number of people along the side.

2. Answer the questions below.

   a. What do you notice about the dots on your graph? What does this mean?

   _____

   _____

   _____

   b. Why might the urban sprawl be good?

   _____

   _____

   c. Why is it bad?

   _____

   _____

The Genetically Modified Organisms Debate

Objectives:

➲ Learn about the controversy behind GMOs and debate both sides in class.

Introduction:

Genetically Modified Organisms (GMOs) are getting a lot of attention these days, but what are they, how do they affect us, and what effect do they have on the environment? Are they safe for the environment? These questions have different answers depending on who you ask. You are going to have an in-class debate about these questions and more.

Procedure:

1. One week before the debate, divide the class into two groups, one in favor of GMOs and one against. You will have one week to prepare your arguments even if they don't match your own belief. Here is some information to get you started:

Genetically Modified Organisms are organisms (plants or animals) that people have changed using DNA (the basic building block inside all living cells) to create a slightly different plant or animal. GMOs are used in biology, medicine, and agriculture. Foods might be genetically modified to prevent pests from eating them, aquarium fish might be modified to be more colorful or even to glow, and people's cells may be modified to help them fight some diseases.

2. Debate your arguments using the following questions to help you get started:

➲ Do you think GMOs should be grown and sold to the general public? Why or why not?

➲ Do you think genetically modified foods that are being sold should be labeled? Why or why not?

➲ Do you think that genetically modified animals should have different rules than genetically modified plants? Why or why not?

➲ Do you think that companies should be able to modify plants so that they cannot produce seeds and therefore farmers must continue to purchase plants from the company?

Does Recycling Really Help?

Objectives:

- ➲ Monitor your garbage production over one week.
- ➲ Calculate the percentage of waste created.
- ➲ Create a plan to reduce your garbage production.

Equipment:

- ➲ 6 bins or bags
- ➲ 6 signs (labeled paper, metal, glass, plastic, organic, and other)
- ➲ garbage production table

Procedure:

1. Label all six bins or bags.
2. On the table make a list of things that should go in each bag.
3. Post a table above each bin or bag.
4. When you put something into a bag, put a tick-mark in the table.
5. Keep track of how many bags of each type of garbage you produce.
6. Compare the number of garbage items and the number of bags and create a pie chart.

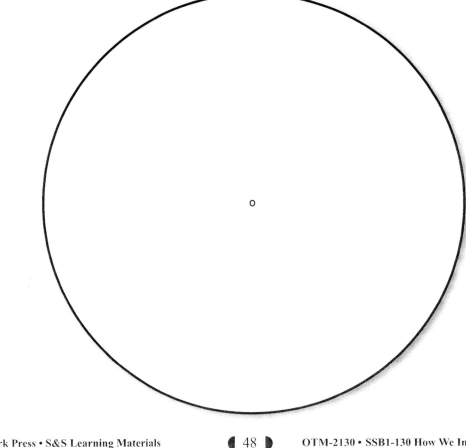

Does Recycling Help?

Extension:

1. Does recycling help?

   _____

   _____

   _____

2. How can you reduce the amount of garbage that goes into the landfills?

   _____

   _____

   _____

Type of Waste: _____

Types of Waste	Number of Items Discarded

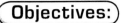

The Greenhouse Effect Game

Objectives:

➲ Feel the heat of the greenhouse effect.
➲ Do an experiment to see how the greenhouse effect works and how it affects the environment.

Introduction:

You may be hearing quite a bit about something called "global warming" these days, maybe on the TV or radio, or from your parents and teachers. But why is it such a big deal? What is it? Should you be worried? Global warming is just what the name says: it's the warming of our planet. It happens very slowly and takes quite a bit of time, but small changes in the Earth's temperature can cause big changes for everything living here. These changes happen because gases get trapped up in the atmosphere (that big layer of gas surrounding our planet, which protects us from the dangers of outer space). Most of the gases up there are important because they keep our planet at a nice temperature. It's all the air pollution we humans are creating that is causing there to be too much gas around our planet. This air pollution comes from the emissions that come out of cars, trucks, and factories and by gases created by cow flatus, farming, and garbage dumps. Together all these gases in our atmosphere spell bad news for us and all living things on this planet.

Experiment #1

Equipment:

➲ blankets
➲ sheets

Procedure:

1. With a bunch of friends, or in your classroom, get everyone to stand or sit huddled closely in a circle.
2. Get an adult or friend to throw a bed sheet over everyone. Try to cover everyone.
3. Now imagine this bed sheet is our atmosphere. What do you notice? *(It's a little warm.)*
4. Now throw a blanket over everyone, leaving the sheet in place.
5. Imagine the blanket is carbon dioxide being pumped into our atmosphere. What do you notice? *(It's getting warmer.)*
6. Add two other blankets for all the other gases. What do you notice? *(It's VERY warm – let us out!)*

 OTM-2130 • SSB1-130 How We Impact the Environment

The Greenhouse Effect Game

Experiment #2

Equipment:
- two large pop bottles without caps
- sunlight
- two thermometers
- data table
- baking soda
- funnel
- vinegar
- spoons
- Plasticine

Procedure:

1. For each pop bottle make a seal around the neck with a piece of Plasticine and push one of the thermometers through until the tip is halfway down each bottle. Label the bottles A and B.
2. Take bottle B and remove the Plasticine cap. Put two tablespoons of baking soda into the bottle. Add about half a cup of vinegar and quickly put the Plasticine and thermometer back over the top.
3. Put both pop bottles in the sun.
4. In your data table, write down the temperature of each bottle.
5. Continue writing down the temperature after every 5 minutes until the end of class.
6. When you have all your data, make a graph to show the change in temperature over time.
7. Write down and discuss your observations. What happened?

Time	start	5	10	15	20	25	30	35	40	45	50	55	60
Temperature of bottle A													
Temperature of bottle B													

Questions:

1. Did you see a difference in temperature change between bottles A and B? _____

2. Explain why or why not?_____
   _____
   _____

3. How does this experiment compare to the real world?_____
   _____

4. What can you do to lower the temperature in bottle B? Can this be done to the world in real life?_____
   _____

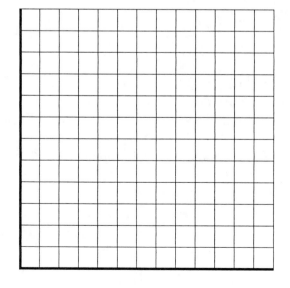

Classroom Composter

Objectives

- Build a classroom composter.
- Learn how food can be recycled.

Equipment:

- large bin with cover
- 1 lb. (454 g) of red wriggler worms
- newspaper
- dirt
- peat moss
- nail and hammer
- water
- calcium carbonate (or crushed egg shells)

Procedure:

1. Have an adult punch holes into the lid of your bin. This will allow air to circulate.

2. Pour equal parts of dirt and peat moss into the empty bin. The dirt mixture should be about 4 inches (10 cm) deep .

3. Tear the newspaper into small pieces. Add this to the dirt mixture and mix well.

4. Add 4 tablespoons (60 ml) of the calcium carbonate to 1 gallon (4 liters) of water. Stir.

5. Pour the water mixture into the bin and mix well making sure not to pack the bedding. The mixture should be fluffy. If the dirt is too wet, leave uncovered to evaporate or add more paper or peat moss. The dirt should be able to be pressed into a ball and hold its shape but not be dripping water.

6. In one corner of the bin add your worms. Make sure to cover them after, they don't like the light.

Using Your Composter: You should feed your worms every two to three days to keep them healthy and happy. When you add food, dig away some dirt, add the food (no more than two cups) and cover it back up with dirt. Add food in a clockwise order around the bin. This way the worms don't have to travel far to get their next meal and by the time you get back to where you started all the food should be gone.

What to Add: Fruits, vegetables, bread, tea, coffee, shredded paper. Do not add anything that contains meat or meat products (such as fats, bones, dairy, oil) or anything with salt or vinegar. For best results, chop all food into small bits before adding them to the composter. This way the food will be digested faster and you will be able to use your bin more often.

Classroom Composter

Problem Solving:

Q. My bin is too wet, what do I do?
A. Open the lid part way and allow the bin to sit in a warm sunny spot. To prevent extra moisture, add more absorbent materials like bread or paper.

Q. My bin is too acidic, what do I do?
A. Add calcium carbonate or crushed egg shells to the bin every 2-3 feedings.

Q. I have a fruit fly problem, what do I do?
A. You should not have a problem with insects unless the food in the bin is not covered properly. Make sure to bury any food you put in the bin and you shouldn't have a problem.

Q. My worms are trying to escape, what do I do?
A. Worms will only try to escape if the conditions in the bin are too moist or acidic. Follow the guidelines above to fix these problems. Also, keep the bin in a well-lit area. Worms are sensitive to light and won't try to leave the darkness of the bin.

Harvesting: After six months or so, your bin will be made up almost entirely of composted organic materials. You will need to harvest the soil created to keep your bin from getting too full.

Procedure:

1. Stop feeding your worms one week before harvesting the dirt.
2. Open the cover so that only half of the bin is covered. Position a bright light over the open side. This will cause the worms to move into the dark so that the dirt can be harvested. Wait 30 minutes.
3. It is best to harvest the dirt outside, as this can be messy. Scoop out the dirt from the open side. There should be very few worms in the dirt.
4. Move the lid so that one quarter of the bin is covered. Wait 30 minutes. Remove the exposed dirt.
5. You can use the remaining quarter bin of dirt to start your next round of composting. Spread the dirt evenly over the bottom, add more peat moss and water just like when you started.
6. If you have too many worms in your bin, remove some and start a second composter or you can set them free outside.

Extensions: Use the following table to measure how much garbage you created before and after starting your composter. Continue recycling as usual.

Amount:	Week 1	Week 2	Week 3	Week 4	Week 5	Week 6	Week 7	Week 8	Week 9	Week 10
garbage										
compost										
paper										
glass, plastic and metal										

Alternate Transportation Challenge

Objective:

➲ Convince people you know to use more environmentally friendly ways to travel.

Procedure:

1. Host an in-class competition to see who is able to convince a person or people to cover the greatest distance without using fuel to get to places they would normally drive or take the bus.

2. You will have one week to convince as many people as you can. You must accompany the people and keep track of the distance covered in the table below.

3. Brainstorm suggestions before starting the competition. You may also need to be convincing. Make sure you know some good reasons why a person should choose to leave their car at home.

4. Choose a prize to be awarded to the winner.

5. Compare ways you convinced people with your classmates. Share problems you faced.

Person	Intended Mode of Transportation	Location Traveled To and From	Alternate Mode of Transportation	Distance Covered
Example: mom	car	home to convenience store	walk	five miles

Packaging Problems

Objectives:

➲ Learn about packaging and how to look for products without too much packaging.
➲ Calculate the waste created by over packaging products.
➲ Design your own environmentally friendly packaging.

Equipment:

➲ calculator
➲ scale
➲ packaged products

Procedure:

1. Find as many packaged products as you can. Make sure to include products that have a lot of packaging and ones that have little packaging. Include food and household items like light bulbs and toothpaste.
2. Weigh the product and packaging and write it down in Column A.
3. Weigh the product by itself and write the weight down in Column B.
4. Calculate the weight of the packaging by subtracting Column B from Column A and write it down in Column C.
5. Calculate the percentage of packaging by dividing Column C by Column A and multiplying by 100.
6. Once you have filled in all the rows, calculate the average by adding up the weight in each column and dividing by the number of products, then multiply by 100.
7. Answer the questions on the following page.

Product	Product and Packaging (A)	Product (B)	Packaging (A-B=C)	Packaging Percent (C/A x 100)
1.				
2.				
3.				
4.				
5.				
6.				
7.				
8.				
9.				
10.				
11.				
12.				
Average (total/12 x 100)				

Packaging Problems

Extension:

1.   What was the average percentage of packaging for the products you examined?

_____

2.   Is this higher or lower than you would expect? Why? _____

_____

3.   Which product has the most packaging? Why do you think it needs so much packaging?

_____

_____

4.   Why is so much packaging used for some products and not others?

_____

_____

5.   Is packaging necessary? Why or why not?

_____

_____

6.   Imagine that you are selling a new product. It's a new kind of mp3 player. Design a packaging for your new gadget. Remember you don't want it to break during shipping and you need to include instructions, batteries, and headphones. You also want to design the most environmentally friendly packaging possible. Describe and draw your design below.

Battery Battle

Objectives:

➲ Learn how to properly dispose of batteries.
➲ Run a battery collection contest at your school.

Procedure:

1. How does a battery work? Label the following diagram, using the resources you have to find the answers.

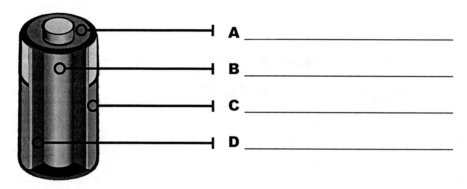

A _____

B _____

C _____

D _____

2. Some parts of the battery are very dangerous. If a battery leaks, the liquid that comes out can burn you. Now, imagine a pile of batteries sitting in a landfill in the hot sun. What's going to happen? Where is all that dangerous stuff going to go?

_____

_____

_____

_____

3. How can you dispose of batteries properly so that this doesn't happen? Can batteries be recycled? How? _____

_____

_____

_____

4. Have a competition in your school to see which class can collect the most batteries for recycling. Every battery that doesn't make it into the landfill is one less battery that's harming the environment. Give each classroom a container to put their batteries in. Make sure they put their classroom number somewhere on the box. Give the classes two weeks to collect as many old batteries as they can. They can collect old batteries from their home, from their parents work, from friends, and from family.

5. Research where batteries can be recycled in your community. Call ahead and tell them about your project and ask if the batteries can be picked up or where to drop them off.

6. Make posters to advertise the competition. Make sure to write why you are collecting batteries and list any prizes that may be awarded.

Battery Battle

7. Find out which class is the winner by weighing the batteries and dividing the weight by the number of students in the class. The class with the most weight per student wins.

8. Announce the winner of the competition and congratulate everyone for participating. Make sure to tell everyone how they have helped the environment.

Extension:

Run this competition every year and compare the numbers of batteries collected each year. Did the number go up? Why do you think this might be? Or did it go down? Why?

Sample Poster:

DON'T THROW BATTERIES IN THE GARBAGE!

CONTEST

CONTEST OPEN TO _____.

COLLECT BATTERIES FOR PROPER DISPOSAL UNTIL _____.

HOW TO PARTICIPATE:

The class that collects the most batteries as measured by the WEIGHT of the batteries DIVIDED by the NUMBER of students in the school WINS _____.

Please assign someone in your class to be responsible for the collection box.

The weighing in of the batteries will happen on _____.

For more information contact _____.

Clearing the Air

Objectives:

➲ Learn what an electrostatic precipitator is and how it works.
➲ Run an experiment to see how the air can be cleaned before being released into the atmosphere.

Equipment:

➲ plastic tube (fluorescent light tube packaging)
➲ wire coat hanger, unfolded
➲ plastic grocery bag
➲ electric blow dryer
➲ punch holes and black pepper
➲ balloon

Introduction:

The air is polluted by a number of different ways. Sometimes gases like carbon dioxide are released into the atmosphere and sometimes tiny particles of contaminants are floating in the air. These tiny particles can be removed from the air by using something called an electrostatic precipitator. These are most often used in power plants, paper mills, and cement plants where a lot of particles can end up floating around in the air.

By doing the experiment below you will see how electrostatic precipitators work.

Procedure:

1. Place one open end of the plastic tube over the pile of punch holes, pepper, etc. and place the hair dryer at the other open end of the tube so that the air will blow across the opening. Turn the blow dryer on. What happens?

   _____

   _____

2. Now, wrap the plastic bag around one end of the unfolded coat hanger and place it inside the plastic tube. Push the coat hanger up and down inside the full length of the tube. Now repeat step 1. What happens now?

   _____

   _____

3. You can try this experiment another way by blowing up a balloon, rubbing it against your hair and then holding the balloon just above the pile of punch holes and pepper. What happens? Why?

   _____

   _____

[adapted from http://web.archive.org/web/20050308115321/www.tnrcc.state.tx.us/air/monops/lessons/precip.html]

Car Craze

Objectives:

⊃ Compare the fuel efficiency of different types of vehicles.
⊃ Research the idling laws in your state/province.
⊃ Observe idling for one week.
⊃ Create an awareness pamphlet for your community.

Procedure:

1. Using the information in the following table, calculate and graph the fuel efficiency of each of the types of vehicles. (Hint: Use a bar graph with the type of vehicle on the x-axis and the fuel efficiency on the y-axis.)

2. Fuel efficiency = distance traveled / amount of gas used

Type of vehicle	Distance traveled with one full tank of gas (miles/km)	Price of gas ($ per gallon/liter)	Cost to fill tank ($)	Amount of gas used (gallons/ liters)	Fuel efficiency (miles/km per 1gallon/liter)
Example	585	3.10	46.50	15	39
Smart car	540	3.20	32.00		
Hybrid car	500	2.95	29.50		
Compact car	430	3.15	31.50		
Hybrid SUV	820	3.10	31.00		
Midsize car	600	3.00	45.00		
Van	680	3.30	66.00		
SUV	620	3.05	61.00		
Pickup truck	750	2.90	72.50		
Hummer	630	3.25	97.50		

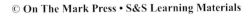

Car Craze

Extension:

1. Research the idling laws in your state or province.

   _____

   _____

2. For one week write down every time you see a car idling and the date that it happened. Idling is when a car is on and running but is not moving.

   _____

   _____

   _____

   _____

3. Discuss your observations with your class.

4. Based on your observations and discussion, make an information pamphlet about idling. Make sure to include why it's bad for the environment, why it is a big problem, and how it can be prevented or reduced. Make copies of this pamphlet and distribute it to friends, family, and neighbors.

Design your pamphlet here.

Are You Energy and Water Efficient?

Objectives:

➲ Take the quiz to find out how energy and water efficient you are and how you can reduce your energy and water usage around the house.

Procedure:

Answer the following questions by circling the object or activity that is more energy or water efficient. Explain your answer.

1. Which light bulbs should I use?

   a) incandescent (regular)   b) compact fluorescent   c) fluorescent tube

   Why? _____

2. At which temperature should I set my thermostat?

   a) 30°C/86°F   b) 25°C/77°F   c) 20°C/68° F

   Why? _____

3. What kind of bathroom tap should I use?

   a) regular   b) low-flow aerator   c) water filter

   Why? _____

4. How should I bathe?

   a) shower   b) bath and shower   c) bath

   Why? _____

5. What color should I paint my walls?

   a) white   b) dark blue   c) doesn't matter

   Why? _____

6. What kind of freezer should I use?

   a) chest freezer   b) upright freezer   c) downright freezer

   Why? _____

7. At what temperature should I set my refrigerator?

   a) -5° to -2°C or 23° to 28°F   b) 2° to 5°C or 36° to 41°F   c) 12° to 15°C or 54° to 59°F

   Why? _____

8. How should I cook my soup?

   a) microwave   b) stove   c) oven

   Why? _____

Are You Energy and Water Efficient?

9. If I'm waiting to pick someone up in a car, what should I do?

   a) turn the car off   b) keep the car running   c) drive around the block

   Why? _____

10. What should I do when I'm brushing my teeth?

    a) turn off the tap   b) keep the tap running   c) use the kitchen sink

    Why? _____

11. When should I water the lawn?

    a) in the morning   b) in the afternoon   c) right after supper

    Why? _____

12. What should I do when I am washing the dishes?

    a) let the water run   b) use a dishwasher   c) use half a sink and rinse afterwards

    Why? _____

13. What should I use to heat my home?

    a) solar power   b) oil   c) natural gas

    Why? _____

Illustrate four ways that you save energy and water in your home in the boxes below.

[adapted from http://www.ecokids.ca/pub/eco_info/topics/energy/energy_efficient/index.cfm]

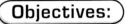

Energy Tradeoff

Objectives:

➲ Learn about alternative energy in the home.
➲ Play a game to show how energy is created and used.

Procedure:

Most homes use hydroelectricity, wood, oil, or natural gas to heat and power their homes, but there are other ways.

1. Working in pairs, imagine that you own a home and that home is in a city, and the city is your classroom.

2. List all the things in your home that use electricity (without looking at the diagram).

3. List all the ways you can think of to power your home (without looking at the diagram).

4. Think of one thing you could do to your home to make it better for the environment.

5. In some cases, if a home produces more energy than it uses it can sell it back to the city for other people to use. Keeping this in mind, how might you change your answer in Step 4?

6. In the table, add your answers from Steps 2 and 3, if they are not already there, and fill in the rows by doing some research.

7. Make a master list for everyone in the class to use. If the prices and energy used do not match, use the average between the different answers.

8. Determine how long you are going to play (30 minutes or for 1 hour).

9. Each "house" will have $10,000 to start. You will need to purchase five things for your home to start, and you will also need to pay your electricity bill.

10. Use the table to figure out how much you can spend.

11. Your teacher will make sure your home is properly equipped, otherwise you might go hungry or get frost bite and need to go to the hospital and pay to get better.

12. Each house can make one additional purchase or sale per round. If you wish to sell something you must sell it to another player, you cannot return it to the store. You can sell it for whatever price you like.

13. At the end of the playing time, every house will calculate how much money they have and how much damage they have done to the environment.

14. The winning team will have the lowest environmental effect. In case of a tie, the person with the most amount of money wins.

Energy Tradeoff

Household Object	Cost to Purchase	Power Used Per Month	Cost to Use Per Month	Environmental Cost Per Month
Oven				
TV				
Air Conditioner				
Heater				
Computer				
Lights				
Refrigerator				
Microwave				
Aquarium				
Printer				
Dish Washer				
Washer				
Dryer				
Water Heater				
Printer				
Alarm Clock				
Stereo system				
Cell phone charger				
Ways to power your home				
Wood				
Hydroelectricity				
Oil				
Natural Gas				
Voltaic Cells (Solar power)				
Wind Turbine				

Understanding Nuclear Energy

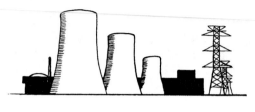

Objective:

➲ Learn how nuclear energy works.

Equipment:

➲ dominos
➲ ruler

Procedure:

1. Follow the pattern shown below to set up half your dominos.

2. With the other half of your dominos, create two straight lines. Make sure they are not too close to the other dominos.

3. Gently push the front domino over from the first set. What happens? Why?

4. Gently push the front domino over from one of the lines of dominos. What happens?

5. Now, place the ruler in the middle of the second line of dominos. Push the first one over. What happens? Why?

6. Read the explanation of nuclear energy below and answer the questions.

What's Happening?

Nuclear power plants use uranium, a radioactive element (have a look at a periodical table to see if you can find it), to create heat and therefore energy through a nuclear fission. Fission happens when one atom of uranium is split into two neutrons (the opposite of fusion). These two neutrons then each hit and split another atom of uranium and so on. Each time there is a collision the number of fissions doubles. The only way to control this chain reaction is to use control rods (the ruler in the exercise above). In a nuclear power plant the control rods are made of cadmium which absorbs neutrons. This stops or controls the number of fissions happening and the amount of energy created.

The problem is that once uranium becomes radioactive it's not possible to make it non-radioactive, and uranium will stay around for a very, very long time. When a nuclear power plant closes down, the uranium is buried deep in the ground in a cadmium barrel, but the uranium can leak and seep into the ground.

Understanding Nuclear Energy

Questions:

1. What is uranium?

   _____

   _____

2. How is energy created from uranium?

   _____

   _____

   _____

3. Why is nuclear energy dangerous?

   _____

   _____

   _____

4. What are the benefits of nuclear energy?

   _____

   _____

   _____

5. Can radioactive material cause mutations in living things?

   _____

   _____

   _____

6. Why are mutations bad?

   _____

   _____

   _____

7. Do you think nuclear energy is good or bad for the environment? (Do more research, if necessary, to answer this question.)

   _____

   _____

   _____

   _____

Industrial Pollution

Objective:

⮞ Learn how factories contribute to air pollution and what can be done.

Procedure:

Big factories pollute in many ways.

Draw a picture of a big factory from your town or from your imagination. Work in groups to discuss how the factory is affecting the environment around it. Use resources to help you find the answers.

Extension:

1. What are the different ways a factory might pollute the environment?

_____

_____

_____

2. What are some of the plants and animals that might be affected by this pollution?

_____

_____

_____

3. How could you make your factory more environmentally friendly?

_____

_____

_____

Improving the Image

Objective:

➲ Identify the problems in the cartoon ecosystem.

Procedure:

1. Circle everything that is environmentally wrong with the picture below.
2. For each thing that is wrong, draw or describe a way to improve the situation, and make the picture more environmentally friendly.

_____

_____

_____

_____

_____

_____

_____

_____

_____

Why Are Invasive Species so Invasive?

Objectives:

- ⊃ Learn about natural selection and how it is important for the survival of different species, including invasive species.
- ⊃ Play a game to learn about competition, adaptation, and extinction.

Equipment:

Seeds:
- ⊃ wheel pasta
- ⊃ kidney beans
- ⊃ paperclips

Beaks:
- ⊃ plastic spoons
- ⊃ magnets (attach a small piece of sticky magnet to a popsicle stick)
- ⊃ paper clips (unfolded)

Other:
- ⊃ plastic cups
- ⊃ masking tape
- ⊃ score chart

Procedure:

1. Break the class into three equal teams. If there is an unequal number, students can switch after each round. Have each team choose a team name (a type of bird).

2. Each team is randomly assigned a beak type. Every "bird" on the team gets one beak and one cup. The cup represents the bird's stomach.

3. Spread the seeds out over a large flat area. There must be enough room for everyone to stand around the "feeding area".

4. Set a feeding time. Forty-five seconds is usually good.

Rules for "birds":

1. Birds must only use their beaks to pick up seeds.

2. Beaks must be held in the non-dominant hand (the hand you don't write with).

3. Cups must be held in the dominant hand.

4. If the cup spills at any time, all seeds are lost.

5. The aim is to pick up as many seeds as possible in the time given.

6. After the feeding time is over, each bird must count his or her seeds by type. The total for the team is written into the Score Chart.

Why Are Invasive Species so Invasive?

7. The team with the fewest seeds eaten loses the bird that collected the fewest seeds. The team with the most seeds eaten gains a bird.

8. Repeat the feeding three or four more times.

9. Now, let's introduce our invasive species. A new bird that has just been released on your island. This bird has a special beak and is able to eat anything. Choose one or two students to be the new bird. These birds will have tape placed around their hand, sticky side out, and they can use their other hand to help remove the seeds. They can collect as many seeds as they want, but they still have to be placed in the cup.

10. Play a couple more rounds with the invasive bird.

11. Once the game is finished, discuss the results.

Extension:

1. Which team lost the most birds? Why?

   _____

2. Which team gained the most birds before the invasive species? Why?

   _____

3. What effect did the invasive bird have on the results? Explain.

   _____

4. Why are invasive species such a big problem?

   _____

5. How can we prevent invasive species from spreading?

   _____

Score Chart		1	2	3	4	5	6	7	8	9	10
Team 1	Wheels										
	Beans										
	Paperclips										
Team 2	Wheels										
	Beans										
	Paperclips										
Team 3	Wheels										
	Beans										
	Paperclips										
Invasive	Wheels										
	Beans										
	Paperclips										

Dealing with Invasive Species

Objectives:
- ⊃ Learn about invasive species.
- ⊃ Come up with a plan to control your invasive species.
- ⊃ Discuss your plan with other groups.

Procedure:

1. Working in groups of two or three, go to **www.invasive.org** and choose an invasive species from one of the lists.
2. Work together to fill in the questions below.
3. Compare your answers to those of the other groups.

Questions:

1. Name of invasive species:_____

2. Reason for choosing this species: _____
   _____
   _____

3. Where did this species come from? _____
   _____

4. How was this species introduced? _____
   _____
   _____

5. Where in North America does this species now live? _____
   _____

6. What does this species eat? _____
   _____

7. What eats it? _____
   _____
   _____

8. Why is it a big problem? _____
   _____
   _____
   _____

9. What could you do to prevent this species from spreading? _____
   _____
   _____
   _____

10. How could we have stopped the introduction of this species? _____
    _____
    _____
    _____

The Zebra Mussel Problem

Objective:

➲ Use logic to learn how zebra mussels spread.

Procedure:

1. Use the clues to solve the spread of the zebra mussel.
2. Use the table below to help you find the answer. Put a dot in the box if both row and column go together and put an X in the box if they don't.
3. Figure out which lake was infected first, by whom, and how.

Logic Clues:

1. Mary did not infect the second lake.
2. Neither Doug nor Mary infected Gray Lake (which was either infected 3rd or 4th).
3. Round Lake (which was infected 1st or 2nd) wasn't infected by the swimmer.
4. The 3rd lake infected wasn't infected by the boater.
5. Neither Mary nor Anna infected the 4th lake.
6. John, the swimmer, infected either the 1st or 2nd lake.
7. Smooth Lake wasn't infected by Doug.
8. Deep Lake was infected by the person who dumped their aquarium water into it.

Logic Problem Table

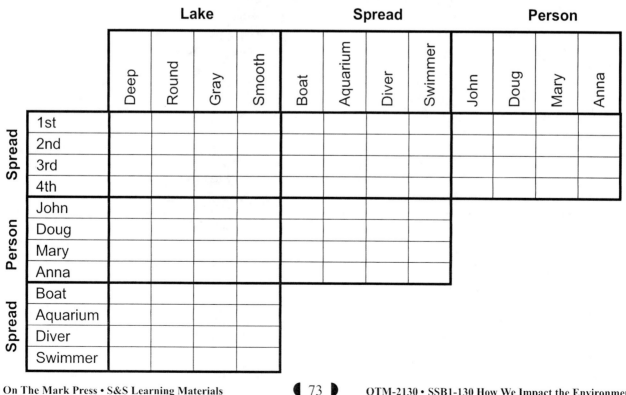

	Lake				Spread				Person			
	Deep	Round	Gray	Smooth	Boat	Aquarium	Diver	Swimmer	John	Doug	Mary	Anna
1st												
2nd												
3rd												
4th												
John												
Doug												
Mary												
Anna												
Boat												
Aquarium												
Diver												
Swimmer												

Endangered Animals Encyclopedia

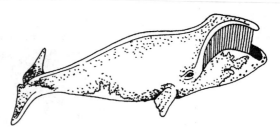

Objectives:

⊃ Learn about endangered animals.
⊃ Share your knowledge with others.

Procedure:

1. Research one endangered animal and create a mini report about it.

2. Your report should be three pages long and should include one picture.

3. Use the section headings on the next page as a guideline for your report. Use as many as possible.

4. Once everyone is done, put all the reports together in alphabetical order and keep it as a classroom endangered animals' encyclopedia.

Extension:

1. Create an electronic or online version of your encyclopedia so that all students can use it at home and at school.

2. Use the information in your book to create a trivia game. Divide the class into teams, and have one person ask questions from the book. Students can use the book to find the answer. The first to respond correctly gets two points. If a team responds incorrectly, they lose a point. The team to finish with the most points wins.

Section Headings

Title	Population
Photo	Distribution
Description	Behavior
Habitats	Communication
Diet	Facts
Enemies	News Articles
Conservation Attempts	References
Reproduction	Classification
History	

Sea Turtle Conservation

Objectives:

- ⊃ Understand the pressures against sea turtle survival.
- ⊃ Play a game to see how chance is a big factor.

Equipment:

- ⊃ identity cards (see following page)
- ⊃ safety pins
- ⊃ three dice
- ⊃ 100 ping-pong balls

Procedure:

1. Have everyone randomly select an identity card and pin it to their shirt.
2. Each person will have a different part to play in this role playing game.

The Game

Part 1:
- ⊃ The turtle must carry all of her eggs and lay them somewhere in the classroom (a basket or bucket can be used as the nest).

Part 2:
- ⊃ The raccoons, poachers, and conservationists will each roll one die to see who gets to the eggs first. High roll wins.
- ⊃ If the raccoons win, they will each roll one die to see how many seconds they will have to collect eggs before they are scared away.
- ⊃ If the poachers win, they collect all the eggs and the game is over.
- ⊃ If the conservationists win, no eggs are lost.

Part 3:
- ⊃ The eggs left in the nest now hatch and the baby turtles start making their way to the ocean. Spread the remaining eggs on the floor.
- ⊃ Now the birds and conservationists each roll one die to see who gets to the eggs first. High roll wins.
- ⊃ If the birds win, they will each roll one die to see how many seconds they will have to collect eggs (now representing hatchlings) before they are scared away.
- ⊃ If the conservationists win, no eggs are lost.

Part 4:
- ⊃ The remaining babies have made it safely to the water.
- ⊃ Now the fish each roll one die to see how many babies they will eat. Each fish will collect the number of balls that is shown on the die.
- ⊃ All the remaining babies grow into juveniles. How many are left?

Sea Turtle Conservation

Part 5:

➲ Now the sharks each roll one die to see how many juveniles they will eat. Each shark will collect the number of balls that is shown on the die.

➲ Now the fishers each roll one die to see how many juveniles they will mistakenly catch in their fishing nets. Each fisher will collect the number of balls that is shown on the die.

How many turtles have survived to adulthood?

Play this game multiple times to see the different outcomes, and discuss the results. You can change the number of each animal/people to see how the numbers or surviving turtles change. Use the table below to record your results.

Trial	Turtles	Raccoons	Poachers	Conservationists	Birds	Fish	Sharks	Fishers	Babies	Adults
1										
2										
3										
4										
5										
6										
7										
8										
9										
10										

North American Endangered Animals

Objective:

➲ Learn about North American animals that are found on the Endangered Species Act list through solving crossword puzzles.

Procedure:

1. Using the clues fill in the crossword with the names of endangered or threatened North American animals.
2. For an added challenge, cover the list of words.

North American Endangered Animals

Clues:

Across:
1. The smallest of the three bears species found in North America.
3. This member of the squirrel family lives in family groups called coteries.
5. This owl hunts during the day.
11. This canine now lives in only three percent of its original home range.
14. Also known as the Duck Hawk.
16. This mammal has large paws that act like snowshoes in deep snow.
18. This large mammal has claws the length of a human finger.
19. This marine mammal is the largest member of the dolphin family.

Down:
2. One of earth's most ancient creatures; this reptile has a beak but no teeth.
4. A wildcat with a short, bobbed tail.
6. Also known as the painted leopard.
7. This reptile kills its prey by performing a "death roll".
8. People used to think that this animal was a mermaid.
9. Also known as a mountain lion.
10. The most primitive of all living seals.
12. The largest member of the canine family.
13. A small, sky-blue bird most often seen flitting around the upper canopy of mature deciduous eastern forests.
14. The Florida _____ is one of the most endangered mammals on earth.
15. A bird that burrows underground.
17. This member of the weasel family is often hunted for its pelt.

Words

American Crocodile	Grey Wolf	Panther
Black Bear	Grizzly Bear	Peregrine Falcon
Bobcat	Hawaiian Monk Seal	Prairie Dog
Burrowing Owl	Killer Whale	Puma
Cerulean Warbler	Lynx	Sea Turtle
Eastern Timber Wolf	Manatee	Snowy Owl
Fisher	Ocelot	

Rainforest Simulation

Objectives:

- Learn about silent extinctions.
- Play a game and discover "new species".

Introduction:

There are millions of species in the rainforests that we still have not discovered. Every time a tree is cut down in the rainforest at least one species we never knew existed goes extinct.

Equipment:

- bristol board (one per group)
- bowl or cup
- various small objects representing insects (the more the better, e.g., paperclips, pennies, metal washers, buttons, dimes, nickels, small beads, large beads, jelly beans, cheerios, thumb tacks, elastic bands, etc.)
- insect cards

Procedure:

1. In the table write each object next to a letter. The letter is the name of the species.
2. In groups of three or four, draw a rainforest on your Bristol board. Look in books or on the Internet to see what a rainforest looks like and what you should draw. Don't forget to include ponds, rivers, bushes, flowers, trees, logs, vines, etc.
3. Following the direction on the cards on the following page, place your "insects" on the appropriate places on your board.
4. Trade places with another group.
5. You are now required to "cut down" some of the trees in the rain forest. To do this, you will use your bowl or cup and with your eyes closed you will place it upside down on your board. The size of your tool will affect your results.
6. Remove all the "insects" that were under your cup. These insects have been killed because of clear-cutting.
7. Repeat the clear-cutting three more times, making sure everyone in the group gets a turn to clear-cut.
8. Once you are finished, count all the remaining insects on your board by species. Write your numbers in the table.
9. Compare your results to the other groups and discuss the following questions.

Questions:

1. Did any of the species go extinct?

2. Did they go extinct for all, most, or only some of the groups?

3. How did the rainforest drawing affect the results?

Rainforest Simulation

Extension:

1. Continue this game by multiplying the number of each insect by two and repeating the game. This represents reproduction over a longer period of time.
2. Keep the number of clear-cuts consistent for each round and each group.
3. Are there some species that do better than others, all the time? Why?
4. Are there some species that stay the same? Why?

Individuals Remaining	Starting Number	Round 1	Round 2	Round 3	Round 4	Round 5	Observations
A	19						
B	3						
C	17						
D	8						
E	2						
F	36						
G	21						
H	13						
I	6						
J	9						
K	20						
L	30						
M	15						
N	15						
O	10						

Species A – lives in tree tops
Species B – lives in ponds
Species C – lives under logs
Species D – lives in bushes and grass
Species E – lives under rocks and logs
Species F – lives in trees and bushes
Species G – lives in flowers
Species H – lives in vines and leaves
Species I – lives in water
Species J – lives under logs
Species K – lives in tree tops
Species L – lives in trees, bushes, flowers and vines
Species M – lives in water and under logs
Species N – lives in water and flowers
Species O – lives in tree bark

Species Identification

Objective: ➲ Learn about biodiversity, why it's important and how to measure it.

Equipment:
➲ hula hoops
➲ rope
➲ yard/meter stick

Introduction:

Before starting this activity, answer the following questions:

1. Why should we care how many species we have in the world?

_____

_____

2. Why do some people devote their entire lives to finding new species?

_____

_____

_____

3. What is conservation? Why is it important?

_____

_____

_____

Everything on earth is interconnected, and these relationships are very complex. If a species becomes extinct many other living things could be affected. But what if we don't even know if it existed in the first place? How do we know which organism we should focus our conservation efforts on?

Procedure:

1. Take a field trip to your local green space or explore your school yard.

2. Conduct a survey of the different organisms in the area using different sampling methods.

   a. **Plants:** Stand in the area that you want to sample. Make sure there is no one standing behind you and then throw the hula hoop behind you. This makes sure that you are sampling a random spot. Now, count all the different plants in the hula hoop. It doesn't matter if you don't know what the plant is called, you can call them A, B, C, etc. Count how many of each you have and write it down in the table. Repeat this 3-5 times per area.

   b. **Birds:** Some scientists use special bird nets to catch, count, and tag birds, but most bird watchers use sight or sound to track what birds are in the area. See how many different bird calls you can identify. How many birds do you see? Write your observations in the table.

Species Identification

c. **Salamanders**: Salamanders like cool, dark, damp places, so you can look under logs and rocks to find them, but depending where you live, you might not find any. The best thing to do if you think salamanders are around but you don't want to hurt the environment they live in is to lay down large square pieces of wood in wet areas. Salamanders will hang out under the boards and you can check on them now and then if they're around.

d. **Insects:** For ground insects it's easiest to look under rocks and logs (make sure to leave the area the way it was before you arrived). Record how many of each type of insects you saw. For flying insects use a pillow case or butterfly net and sweep it across the leaves of bushes and grass. Identify and count the insects you catch.

e. **Trees:** To sample trees choose an area and define it by making a circle with the rope. Have someone stand in the middle of the area and hold on to one end of the rope. Have another person hold the other end of the rope and walk in a circle, keeping the rope tight. Every time the rope hits a tree, stop and identify the trees and count how many of each are in the area.

3. Using the sample table provided, report your findings to your local nature society or museum.

Plants		Birds		Salamanders		Insects		Trees	
Species	Number	Species	Number	Species	Number	Species	Number	Species	Number

Protecting the World's Animals

Objectives:

➲ Identify recently extinct animal species.
➲ Research environmental organizations.
➲ Create your own environmental organization.

Procedure:

1. Name five animals that have gone extinct in the past 100 years. How did it happen?

   a. _____

   b. _____

   c. _____

   d. _____

   e. _____

2. What could have been done to prevent the extinction of these animals?

   a. _____

   b. _____

   c. _____

   d. _____

   e. _____

3. Research three environmental organizations that work to prevent extinction. List them and their main goals.

   a. _____

   b. _____

   c. _____

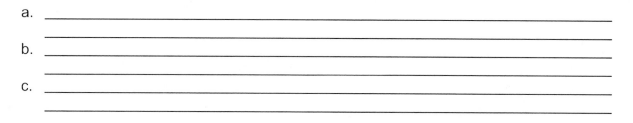

Protecting the World's Animals

4. Design your own environmental organization, answering the following questions:

   a. What will it be called? _____
   b. What would the logo look like? Draw your logo in the box.
   c. How many members will you start with? _____
   d. What will be your organization's main goals? _____

   _____
   _____
   _____
   _____

5. What areas of the environment will you aim to protect?

   _____
   _____
   _____
   _____

6. How will you spread awareness about endangered or threatened animals?

   _____
   _____
   _____
   _____

7. How will you fund your organization?

   _____
   _____
   _____
   _____

8. What kind of research will you do?

   _____
   _____
   _____
   _____

9. How will you get the community involved in your organization?

   _____
   _____
   _____

Antibiotic Resistance

Objective:

➲ Learn why sometimes too much medicine can be bad.

Procedure:

➲ Read the story below, then answer the questions and solve the mystery

Marisha was very worried about getting sick. She was very worried because she seemed to get sick all the time. It was never anything serious, sometimes just a cold and other times she would get the flu. Whenever she felt like she might be coming down with something she would go to her doctor and ask for antibiotics because she knew that antibiotics would kill the bad bacteria in her body and make her feel better. One day, in between cold and flu season, Marisha got a throat infection. This was something she hadn't had before. She again went to her doctor and asked for antibiotics. She took her medicine like she was told, but her sore throat didn't get any better. It felt ten times worse than any cold or flu she had ever had and nothing seemed to get rid of her infection. She eventually got better, but it took a long time, and she felt very bad for a very long while.

Questions:

What happened? Why didn't her usual medication work? If you can't figure it out, try answering the clue questions below by using your dictionary, the resource centre, or the Internet to help you solve the mystery.

Clues:

1. What is a cold?_____
_____

2. What is the flu? _____
_____

3. What is an infection? _____
_____

4. What are antibiotics? _____
_____

5. What are bacteria? _____
_____

6. What is a virus? _____
_____

7. Are bacteria bad for you? Why or why not? _____
_____

8. Are viruses bad for you? Why or why not? _____
_____

9. What is antibiotic resistance? _____
_____

Antibiotic Resistance

Extension:

If you still need help figuring out this mystery, see if you can explain what is happening in each of the cartoons below:

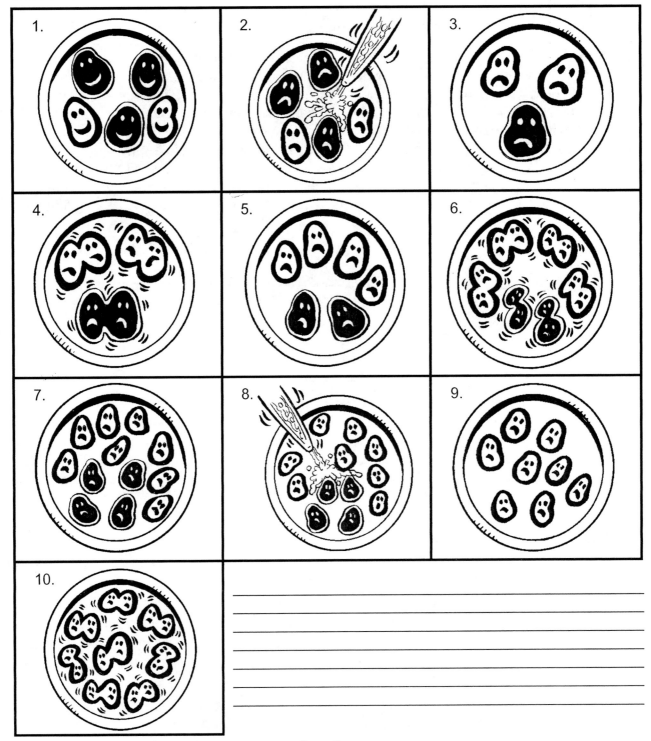

Does the Government Care?

Objectives:

➲ Understand what the Kyoto Protocol is.
➲ Write a letter to the government.

Procedure:

A. Answer the following questions:

1. What is the Kyoto Protocol?
   _____
   _____

2. Why is North America having such a hard time meeting it?
   _____
   _____

3. What is being done by your government to reduce greenhouse gas emissions?
   Is it enough? _____

4. How can you reduce your own greenhouse gas emissions?
   _____
   _____

5. How can your small changes be used to make a big difference?
   _____
   _____

6. What will happen if little or nothing is done to change the way we use our resources?
   _____
   _____

7. Why are other countries able to meet the Kyoto Protocol?
   _____
   _____

8. Do you think the Kyoto Protocol is fair for all countries involved?
   _____
   _____

9. Do you think the Kyoto Protocol can be achieved? Why or why not?
   _____
   _____
   _____

B. Use your answers and your knowledge (do some research if you don't know much about it) to write a letter to your local government, voicing your concern. Tell them why you think change needs to happen and what should be done. Be polite, and make sure that your suggestions are possible. Make sure to include your home or school address so that you can be sent a reply. Write your letter in rough and then ask your teacher for permission to write it on your school's official stationery.

Projecting into the Future

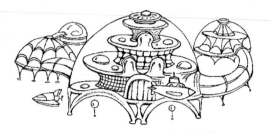

Objectives:

⊃ Imagine what the future will look like.

Procedure:

1. Imagine yourself 50 years in the future.
2. What do you think the world will look like?
3. Write a story, taking everything you have learned so far into consideration.
4. Use the questions below to help you imagine the future world.
5. Draw a picture to accompany your story.
6. Present your visualization to the class.

Helpful Questions:

1. Will the world be a better place or not?
2. How will we harvest energy?
3. What will our mode of transportation be?
4. How friendly will the environment/ weather be?
5. What will the cities look like?
6. What will the ocean look like?
7. What will the landscape look like?
8. What will children do for fun?
9. Will people work the same jobs?
10. What will we use to heat our homes?
11. What diseases will still be around?
12. How much poverty will there be?
13. Will homes be different?

In 50 years, I think the world will… _____

_____

_____

_____

_____

_____

_____

In 50 years, I think the world will look like this:

Money Madness

Objectives:

⊃ Identify the costs and benefits of being environmentally friendly.
⊃ Create an environmental budget.

Procedure:

1. In the table below, write down all the pros and cons to environmental responsibility. An example has been given.
2. Use the resources available to you to estimate a cost for each.
3. At the bottom of each column, add the total costs.
4. Compare the overall monetary pros and cons. Answer the questions below.

Environmental Pros		Environmental Cons	
Description	Cost	Description	Cost
example: Limiting garbage	$0.36/bag	Not conserving household electricity	$100/month
Total cost of pros		Total cost of cons	

Extension:

1. Which is higher? Why? _____
_____
_____

2. How can you decrease the cost of being environmentally friendly?
_____
_____
_____

3. Will the cost decrease over time? Why or why not? _____
_____
_____

4. Is being environmentally friendly more expensive for the government or for the citizens? Why? _____
_____
_____

Conclusion

Based on the results of the survey you created in the first activity, do you think the people in your community understand the impacts they are having on the environment? If your answer is no, how can you make people more aware? As a class, summarize the information you collected from this survey in the form of a brochure. Distribute the brochure to people in your community including the people who filled out the survey. Also include tips on how people can help reduce their impact. Some examples might include:

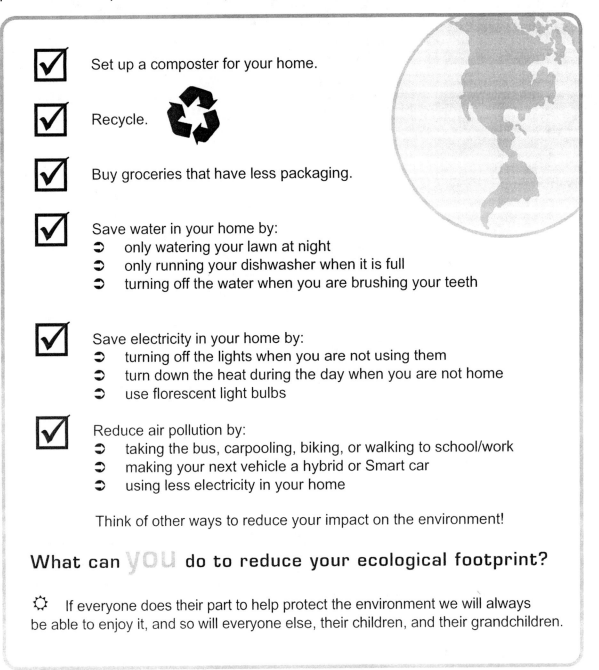

☑ Set up a composter for your home.

☑ Recycle.

☑ Buy groceries that have less packaging.

☑ Save water in your home by:
- ➲ only watering your lawn at night
- ➲ only running your dishwasher when it is full
- ➲ turning off the water when you are brushing your teeth

☑ Save electricity in your home by:
- ➲ turning off the lights when you are not using them
- ➲ turn down the heat during the day when you are not home
- ➲ use florescent light bulbs

☑ Reduce air pollution by:
- ➲ taking the bus, carpooling, biking, or walking to school/work
- ➲ making your next vehicle a hybrid or Smart car
- ➲ using less electricity in your home

Think of other ways to reduce your impact on the environment!

What can you do to reduce your ecological footprint?

✪ If everyone does their part to help protect the environment we will always be able to enjoy it, and so will everyone else, their children, and their grandchildren.

Answer Key

Positive, Negative or Neutral? (Page: 17)

Air pollution – Negative, because all the pollution we pump into the air creates greenhouse gases which cause global warming, and only trees can reverse the effects of air pollution.

Fishing – Negative, if over-fishing, because the fish cannot reproduce fast enough to replenish the fish lost; neutral, if fishing sustainably and in an environmentally friendly way.

Land Use – Neutral, if used in a environmentally friendly way; negative, if too much run-off, deforestation, and nutrient leaching occurs.

Mining – Negative, because many toxic chemicals are used to extract or clean the minerals and these chemicals can leak into the environment causing all sorts of problems.

Waste Treatment – Positive, because we can speed up the process of decomposition.

Water Treatment – Positive, because we can reuse water instead of always using a fresh supply.

Recycling – Positive, because we can reduce the amount of waste we produce by reusing materials like plastic, paper, and metal.

Tree Planting – Positive, because trees help clean the air, provide homes for many animals, and are important for the environment.

Hunting – Negative, if hunting irresponsibly, poaching, or exceeding your limit. Neutral, if hunting responsibly. People killed off many natural predators so too many deer and moose are using up the forest resources, and now we must act as the predators. An alternative would be to reintroduce natural predators.

Dredging for Oil – Negative, because we are constantly depleting our oil reserves and causing oil spills in our oceans and on our land, and causing pollution by using oil to fuel our vehicles and to heat our homes.

The Efficiency of Fishing (Page: 22)

14. a) The net and bottom trawler could both be the fastest.

b) These results may vary, but you should notice that the hook and line takes the longest and only catches large fish, and the net takes the shortest amount of time, but won't catch many bottom feeders. The bottom trawler can quickly catch everything. Because bottom trawlers catch everything so easily, fishers don't have to spend as much time fishing, but they also catch many things they don't need (like sea turtles and dolphins which often die from their injuries) and they destroy the bottom of the ocean by dragging their nets across the bottom.

Purple Loosestrife and Wetlands (Page: 23)

1. A wetland is a natural ecosystem made up of very wet soil where plants that need a lot of water typically grow. Water movement is reduced in these areas and is naturally filtered by the soil and organisms in the wetland.

2. Bog – very acidic soil; swamp – a deep wetland with more open area than a marsh, dominated by trees and bushes; marsh – similar to a swamp but dominated by low growing plants; mangrove – a salt water wetland dominated by mangrove-specific trees; bayou – a creek flowing through a swamp.

3. mallard duck, stickleback fish, mangrove trees, water moccasins

5. Europe, Africa, Australia, and Asia

6. It was probably imported by ships traveling overseas with muddy water in the ballast tanks which contained Purple Loosestrife seeds.

7. Disruption of water flow in rivers and wetlands, less biodiversity because native species are crowded out, change in life cycles of birds, amphibians, and algae. High absorption of water causing wetlands to dry out.

8. It produced many seeds which can travel in the wind great distances, and a new plant can grow from a small piece of root left in the soil.
9. three million
10. Scientists discovered beetles that eat purple loosestrife and are using it to control its spread. There are four types of beetles that can control its spread: two species of leaf beetles and two species of weevils.
11. People fill in wetlands to make parking lots or farm land or flood them to make recreational lakes; common carp.

Testing for Contaminants (Page: 26)
1. The different chemicals test for different things. No one chemical can test for everything. You could use more than two chemicals, but for this experiment we only needed two.
2. Color will vary depending on amount of contamination and the type of fertilizer and pesticides used.
5. The indicators detect the acidity of the water. Water has a pH of around 7 which means that it's neither acidic nor basic. If the water has been contaminated the pH will change causing the indicators to change color.

Local Water Treatment (Page: 27)
   Diagram: from drain to storage tanks where sedimentation occurs, sediment goes to landfill, water goes through filter, then to a tank where it is disinfected, cleaned, and treated, to reservoir where it is redistributed and comes out of the tap.

Building Dams (Page: 30)
1. From dams, wind generators, solar panels, nuclear fission.
2. A dam is a barrier in the water that creates two levels of water.
3. Beavers build dams as protection from predators and weather and so that they can have easy access to food in the winter.
4. Both a hydroelectric dam and a beaver dam divide the water and cause flooding, but a hydroelectric dam is used to create electricity, is built by people, and is often built in places that can't benefit from flooding. Beavers build their dams in marshlands or swamps, and the flooding helps create new or bigger wetlands.
6. They can be good because the energy created is cleaner than using oil or coal, but it's bad because it destroys habitats through flooding and changes the environment around it.
7. Dams cause flooding upriver and reduce water levels downriver. These changes affect the animals and plants living in the area, and often cause many shoreline habitats to be destroyed. It also affects the movement of water so that fish and other water creatures cannot freely move up or down river. The temperature of the water can also be affected.
8. a) People living close to the river may have to move to avoid flooding.
   b) Animals will lose their shoreline homes and fish migration will be restricted.
   c) Shoreline plants will be destroyed.

Erosion (Page: 33)
5b) Shorelines (lakes, oceans, rivers), in the Arctic when glaciers move against the ground, anywhere there is dirt than can be moved by wind, water, or ice.
c) Erosion is what turns rock into sand, and allows new dirt to replace old. It keeps the soil moving and mixes nutrients and minerals into the soil, making it healthier for plants. Water erosion allows water to absorb important nutrients too.
d) Human-caused erosion can be bad because important land can be lost to the lakes and oceans and causes coastal habitats to be destroyed. Also, erosion near farms can cause fertilizer and pesticides to enter the water.

How Do Trees Clean the Air? (Page: 37)

2. a) 8,629 trees
   b) 48 trees
   c) 354 trees
   d) 72 trees

Fretting Over Fertilizer (Page: 38)

Procedure 1:

3. Fertilizer is a substance that is used on plants to make them grow faster.
4. Fertilizer provides plants with nitrogen, phosphorus, and potassium which are chemicals a plant needs but that are often only available in small amounts in the soil.
5. The fertilizer is either sold, thrown in the garbage, or stored for later.
7. If there is too much fertilizer too much of these important chemicals will be absorbed into the ground or end up in the water and can cause poisoning to plants and animals.

Procedure 2:

1. The third plant is a control. Scientists use a control so that they can compare the experimental plant with the one that has nothing unusual done to it.
2. You want to make sure that all the plants have the same amount of sunlight and each get the same amount of time in each position, just in case one position is better than another.
3. You don't want the amount of fertilizer used to affect your results.

The Effects of Recreational Vehicles on the Environment (Page: 41)

ATVing – Marshlands are very sensitive to disturbances, and an ATV driving carelessly by a beaver dam could cause the beavers to flee and never come back; the wild flowers could be crushed and destroyed by the ATV. Driving off trail can destroy many plants, animals, and animal homes, and driving through the water can cause damage to the aquatic ecosystem. Monarch butterflies are very sensitive to disturbances as well, and will fly away before having fed enough to get them through the next part of their long journey and they may not survive.

Motor Boating – Boating too fast on small rivers can cause erosion, which can destroy heron and other birds nesting areas. Again, marshes are sensitive to disturbances and can be damaged by fast moving waters or oil or gasoline that might leak from the boat. Turtles who float on the water could get hit by the propellers of the boat and be injured or killed. A no fishing sign usually means that the area is protected: no harm may come from boating through the area, but boats shouldn't move too quickly.

The Urban Sprawl (Page: 46)

2a) They curve to the right, meaning that the number of people is decreasing as you get further from the centre of the city.
b) It means that people get to own houses and have land and not have to live directly in a city, but they are close enough to the city that they can work in and visit the city any time they want.
c) This means that more land is used to house people than is necessary and more resources are used to build, heat, and provide electricity to these homes. It also means that more people are driving through traffic to work and are using large amounts of fuel.

Battery Battle (Page: 57)

2. The sun and rain will cause the batteries to leak and the chemicals will leak into the soil and eventually into the water where they could make people and other animals very sick.
3. People should use rechargeable batteries so that fewer batteries are thrown out and batteries can be sent to be recycled. The metal in the batteries can be recycled and the corrosive chemicals can be disposed of properly.

Car Craze (Page: 60)

Type of vehicle	Distance traveled with one full tank of gas (miles/km)	Price of gas ($ per gallon/ liter)	Cost to fill tank ($)	Amount of gas used (gallons / liters)	Fuel efficiency (miles/km per 1gallon/liter)
Example	585	3.10	46.50	15	39
Smart car	540	3.20	32.00	10	54
Hybrid car	500	2.95	29.50	10	50
Compact car	430	3.15	31.50	10	43
Hybrid SUV	820	3.10	31.00	20	41
Midsize car	600	3.00	45.00	15	40
Van	680	3.30	66.00	20	34
SUV	620	3.05	61.00	20	31
Pickup truck	750	2.90	72.50	25	30
Hummer	630	3.25	97.50	30	21

Are You Energy and Water Efficient? (Page: 62)

1. b) Compact fluorescent bulbs use one-quarter of the energy of a regular light bulb and last up to 10 times longer.
2. c) This is a comfortable temperature and you save electricity. If you're cold, put on another sweater.
3. b) These taps use less water but add air to the stream so that the pressure and amount seem the same as a regular tap.
4. a) A quick shower saves more water than running a bath.
5. a) White reflects light making your room seem brighter so that you don't have to use as much light.
6. a) A chest freezer doesn't warm up as fast as other freezers when you open it.
7. b) Anything colder and your food will freeze, anything warmer and your food will go bad.
8. b) Using the stove uses less energy than the microwave or oven.
9. a) Idling uses gas and causes unneeded pollution.
10. a) If you're not using the water turn off the tap.
11. a) Because it's cooler in the morning, less water is needed because it doesn't evaporate as fast.
12. c) Use as little water as possible.
13. a) Solar power is completely renewable and does not pollute.

Understanding Nuclear Energy (Page: 67)

1. Uranium is an element that can be made radioactive to create energy.
2. Energy is created by splitting the neutrons of uranium which releases energy in the form of heat.
3. Because uranium is radioactive it can cause damaging mutations in living things.
4. Nuclear energy is very clean energy, as long as the power plant is running.
5. Yes!
6. Not all mutations are bad, but a lot of mutations are. They can cause things like cancers and deformities in babies.

Industrial Pollution (Page: 68)

1. Factories can pollute the water, the air, and the soil.
2. Fish, birds, insects, mammals, reptiles, amphibians, all nearby animals.
3. Filter the air and water that is being released. Control the temperature of the water being released. Don't build a factory close to sensitive ecosystems. Use alternate energy to power your factory.

Improving the Image (Page: 69)

Put the litter in a trashcan, put a filter on the smoke stack of the factory, patch the leaky ship, turn off the idling car, plant another tree next to the one being cut down, put up a "No ATVing" sign, turn the lights off in the house where there is no one inside the room, turn the abandoned lot into a park, add a water treatment plant to clean up the sewer water before it enters the water.

The Zebra Mussel Problem (Page:73)

1st – Mary infected Round Lake with her boat
2nd – John infected Smooth Lake by swimming
3rd – Anna infected Grey Lake by diving
4th – Doug infected Deep Lake with his aquarium

North American Endangered Animals (Page:77)

See page 96 for answers to crossword puzzle.

Species Identification (Page: 81)

1. We don't even know how many species exist on this plant. Each one is unique and specially adapted for its environment. There is a lot to learn about all of these animals, and by studying them we can gain a better understanding of how the world works.
2. People are discovering new species all the time. Scientists know how important it is to learn about the new creatures they find, and discovering new species is a very exciting thing to do.
3. Conservation is the protection of organisms and their habitat. Conservationists tend to focus on plants and animals that are endangered or threatened and they work to protect these organisms so that they don't go extinct. They also help spread awareness about the organisms they are protecting.

Protecting the World's Animals (Page: 83)

1. Hint: Explore http://extinctanimals.petermaas.nl/

Antibiotic Resistance? (Page: 86)

1. Dark cells are normal. White cells are antibiotic resistant.
2. Antibiotic is added.
3. Normal cells are killed.
4. More space and resources are available for the antibiotic resistant cells to grow.
8. Antibiotics are added again.
9. All normal cells are killed.
10. Antibiotic resistant cells take over. A new antibiotic is needed to kill these antibiotic resistant bacteria.

Does the Government Care? (Page: 87)

1. The Kyoto Protocol is an initiative set up by the United Nations to globally reduce the amount of greenhouse gases released into the atmosphere.

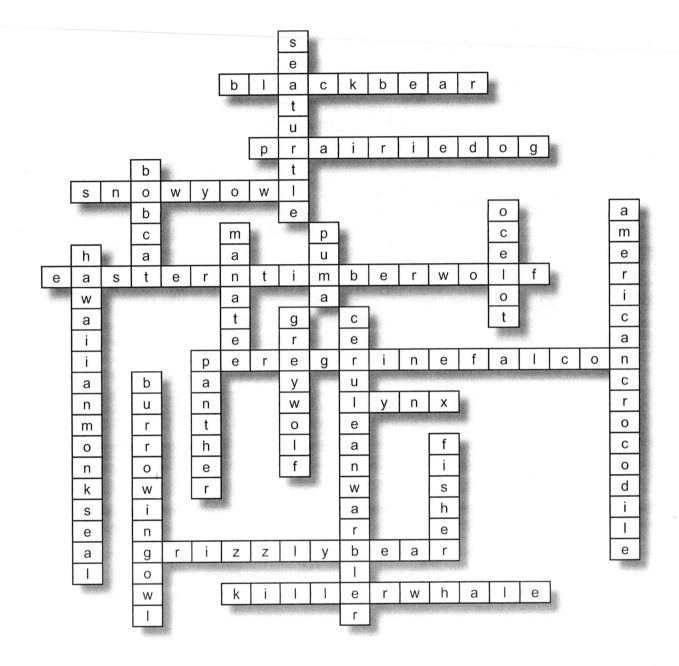